Benson John Lossing, John Trumbull

M'Fingal

An Epic Poem

Benson John Lossing, John Trumbull
M'Fingal
An Epic Poem

ISBN/EAN: 9783744704830

Printed in Europe, USA, Canada, Australia, Japan

Cover: Foto ©ninafisch / pixelio.de

More available books at **www.hansebooks.com**

BY JOHN TRUMBULL.

WITH INTRODUCTION AND NOTES

BY BENSON J. LOSSING, LL.D.,

AUTHOR OF "PICTORIAL FIELD-BOOK OF THE REVOLUTION," ETC., ETC.

NEW YORK:
AMERICAN BOOK EXCHANGE,
764 BROADWAY.
1881.

INTRODUCTION.

The scenes and incidents of the old war for independence, known as the American Revolution, furnished themes for contemplation and comment for every variety of minds, and evolved many brilliant sparks of genius which might otherwise have remained latent in the flint of common thought. While the powers of highest statesmanship and military skill were demanded in the management of great public interests, there appeared much in the details of current events to excite mirth and provoke the keenest weapons of wit and satire to wonderful activity. Prudence generally commended anonymity to those who used the Press for the exercise of these weapons, at a time when there was an enemy in every bush. But such active men as

Paine, Hopkinson, Freneau, Trumbull, and others of less note, could not long wear the disguise so as effectually to conceal themselves, and they became objects of admiration for the Patriots, and of hatred for the Loyalists.

Of all the literary productions of that day, having for its theme the character and doings of the men and times of the Revolution, the remarkable epic entitled M'FINGAL is confessedly most deserving of immortality. It holds an honorable place among works of highest poetic merit; and as a satire, applied with scathing power to those who opposed the war, and were active in their loyalty to the king, it exhibits force rarely equalled, and never surpassed by its predecessors in that peculiar field. That force can be appreciated now, when almost three generations of men have passed away since the actors in the drama were upon the stage, only by a thorough knowledge of the point of each allusion, drawn from the character of the times, and familiarity with the social and political position of the victims of the keen Damascene blade of the satirist.

The late Timothy Dwight, President of Yale College, who was a compatriot, a brother poet, and a friend of the author, writing in long-after years, said : "It may be observed, without any partiality, that M'Fingal is not inferior in wit and humor to Hudibras; and in every other respect is superior. It has a regular plan, in which all the parts are well proportioned and connected. The subject is fairly proposed, and the story conducted through a series of advancements and retardations to a catastrophe, which is natural and complete. The versification is far better, the poetry is in several instances in a good degree elegant, and in some even sublime. It is also free from those endless digressions, which, notwithstanding the wit discovered in them, are so tedious in Hudibras; the protuberances of which are a much larger mass than the body on which they grow."

"The Hudibrastic body," says the *Cyclopædia of American Literature*, "is thoroughly interpenetrated by its American spirit. The illustrations, where there were the greatest temptations to plagiarism, are drawn from the writer's own biblical and classical reading, and the colloquial familiarities of the times. For the manners of the poem, there is no record of the period which supplies so vivid a presentation of the old Revolutionary Whig habits of thinking and acting. We are among the actors of the day—the town committees, the yeomanry, the politicians and soldiers, participating in the rough humors of the times; for nothing is more characteristic of the struggle than a certain vein of pleasantry and hearty animal spirits which entered into it. Hardships were endured with fortitude, for which there was occasion enough, but the contest was carried on with wit as with other weapons."

The purpose of the poem was explained by the author himself, in a letter to the Marquis de Chastellux, written in 1785. "It had been undertaken," he said, "at the instigation of some of the leading members of the first Congress, who urged him to compose a satirical poem on the events of the campaign in the year 1775;" and that he "had aimed at expressing, in a poetical manner, a general account of the American contest, with a particular description of the character and manners of the times, interspersed with anecdotes, which no history could probably record or display; and where as much impartiality as possible, satirize the follies and extravagancies of his countrymen, as well as of their enemies. I determined," he says, "to describe every subject in the manner it struck my own imagination, and without confining myself to a perpetual effort at wit, drollery and humor, indulge every variety of manner, as my subject varied, and insert all the ridicule, satire, sense, sprightliness and elevation, of which I was master." How well this design was executed, the intelligent reader will discover.

The first and second cantos of M'Fingal were published as one, in a thin pamphlet of forty pages, by William and Thomas Bradford, of Philadelphia. It was issued in the Autumn of 1775, as *Canto I., or the Town-Meeting*. In the course of the next year it was reprinted in London, where it passed through several editions, and was very popular with the anti-ministerial party in Great Britain and America. For a long time it was believed to be the production of some English scholar, and made a very favorable impression everywhere, on account of its literary merits. As a political satire it was regarded as inimitable, and was praised by men of all parties. But when it was known that the author was a native of New England, the London press and loyal writers in

America, poured obloquy and contempt upon him in full measure.

When the first part of M'Fingal was published, the author had sketched a plan for its extension, but he did not take it up again until the close of the war, when his friends urged him to complete it. He did so, by dividing the first half into two cantos, and adding two more. The whole work was printed and published by Hudson and Godwin at Hartford in Connecticut, before the close of 1782. Of that edition the one now offered to the public is a faithful transcript.

In the explanatory notes appended to the Poem in the present edition, the reader will find that full information which is necessary to a proper appreciation of the force of the satire.

John Trumbull, the author of M'FINGAL, was the child of a congregational minister. He was an only son, delicate in physical constitution, and a favorite of his accomplished mother. He was an exceedingly precocious child, and at the age of seven years was considered qualified to enter Yale College, as a student. There he was graduated, in 1767, with the degree of Bachelor of Arts, and remained a student three years longer. He turned his attention chiefly to polite literature, as well as the Greek and Latin classics, and became a most accomplished scholar. He and Timothy Dwight became intimate friends, and the bond of mutual attachment was severed only by death. They were co-essayists, in 1769; and, in 1771, they were both appointed tutors in the college. The following year young Trumbull published the first part of a poem entitled *The Progress of Dulness*. He selected the law as his profession, and devoted much of his leisure time to its study. He was admitted to the bar in 1773, but immediately afterward went to Boston, and placed himself under the instructions of John Adams. While in Boston he wrote an *Elegy on the Times*, a poem in sixty-eight stanzas, which celebrated the Boston Port Bill, the non-importation associations, and the present strength and future glory of the country. He commenced the practice of law at Hartford, in 1781, and soon became distinguished for legal acumen and forensic eloquence. As we have observed, his *M‘Fingal* was completed, and published at Hartford in 1782. As authors were then unprotected by copyright laws, there were more than thirty different pirated impressions printed, and circulated by "newsmongers, hawkers, peddlers, and petty chapmen."

Mr. Trumbull was soon afterward associated with Humphreys, Barlow, and Dr. Lemuel Hopkins, in the production of a work which they styled *The Anarchiad*. It contained bold satire, and exerted considerable influence on the popular taste.

In 1789, Mr. Trumbull was appointed State Attorney for the county of Hartford; and, in 1792, he represented that district in the Connecticut legislature. His health failed; and, in 1795, he resigned his office, and declined all public business. Toward the close of 1798, a severe illness formed the crisis of his nervous excitement, and after that his health was much better. He was again elected to a seat in the State legislature in May, 1800, and the following year he was appointed a judge of the Superior Court of Connecticut. From that time he abandoned party politics, as inconsistent with judicial duties. In 1808, he was appointed judge of the Supreme Court of Errors, in which office he remained several years. In the year 1805, Woodruff and Periam printed an edition of M'Fingal at Elizabethtown, in New Jersey, by permission of the author. In 1820, he revised his works, and they were published in Hartford, in handsome style, by Samuel G. Goodrich, from whom the author received the handsome compensation of one thousand dollars.

Judge Trumbull and his wife went to Detroit in 1825, and made their abode with their daughter, Mrs. Woodbridge, where he died of gradual decay, on the 10th of May, 1831, at the age of eighty-one years.

M'FINGAL:

A MODERN

EPIC POEM,

IN FOUR CANTOS.

Ergo non satis est risu diducere rictum
Auditoris: et est quædam tamen hic quoque virtus;
Est brevitate opus, ut currat sententia, neu se
Impediat verbis lassas onerantibus aures.
Et sermone opus est modo tristi, sæpe jocoso,
Defendente vicem modo Rhetoris, atque Poetæ,
Interdum urbani parcentis viribus atque
Extenuantis eas consulto.   Ridiculum acri
Fortius et melius magnas plerumque secat res.
                    Horat. Lib. 1. Sat. 10.

HARTFORD:
Printed by Hudson and Goodwin, near the
Great Bridge, 1782.

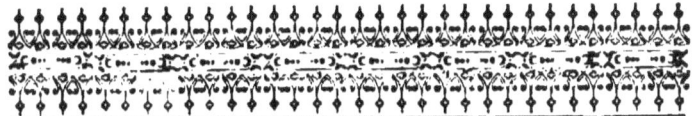

M'FINGAL:

CANTO FIRST,

OR

The TOWN-MEETING, A. M.

WHEN Yankies[1], fkill'd in martial rule,
Firſt put the Britiſh troops to ſchool;
Inſtructed them in warlike trade,
And new manœuvres of parade;
The true war-dance of Yanky-reels,
And manual exerciſe of heels;
Made them give up, like faints complete,
The arm of fleſh and truſt the feet,
And work, like Chriſtians undiſſembling,
Salvation out, by fear and trembling[2];
Taught Percy faſhionable races,
And modern modes of Chevy-chaces:

From

From Boston, in his best array,
Great 'Squire M'Fingal' took his way,
And graced with ensigns of renown,
Steer'd homeward to his native town.

His high descent our heralds trace
To Ossian's famed Fingalian race:
For tho' their name some part may lack,
Old Fingal spelt it with a Mac;
Which great M'Pherson, with submission
We hope will add, the next edition [b].

His fathers flourish'd in the Highlands
Of Scotia's fog-benighted islands;
Whence gain'd our 'Squire two gifts by right,
Rebellion and the Second-sight [c].
Of these the first, in ancient days,
Had gain'd the noblest palms of praise,
'Gainst Kings stood forth and many a crown'd head
With terror of its might confounded;
Till rose a King with potent charm
His foes by goodness to disarm,

Whom

Whom ev'ry Scot and Jacobite⁷
Straight fell in love with, at firſt ſight;
Whoſe gracious ſpeech, with aid of penſions,
Huſh'd down all murmurs of diſſenſions,
And with the ſound of potent metal,
Brought all their bluſt'ring swarms to ſettle⁸;
Who rain'd his miniſterial mannas,
Till loud Sedition ſung hoſannahs;
The good Lords-Biſhops and the Kirk
United in the public work⁹;
Rebellion from the Northern regions,
With Bute and Mansfield ſwore allegiance¹⁰;
And all combin'd to raze as nuiſance,
Of church and ſtate, the conſtitutions;
Pull down the empire, on whoſe ruins
They meant to edify their new ones;
Enſlave th' American wilderneſſes,
And tear the provinces in pieces¹¹:
For theſe our 'Squire among the valiant'ſt,
Employ'd his time and tools and talents;
And in their cauſe with manly zeal
Uſed his firſt virtue, to rebel;

And

And found this new rebellion pleasing
As his old king-destroying treason.

Nor less avail'd his optic sleight,
And Scottish gift of second-sight.
No antient sybil fam'd in rhyme
Saw deeper in the womb of time [12];
No block in old Dodona's [13] grove,
Could ever more orac'lar prove.
Nor only saw he all that was,
But much that never came to pass;
Whereby all Prophets far outwent he,
Tho' former days produc'd a plenty;
For any man with half an eye,
What stands before him may espy;
But optics sharp it needs I ween,
To see what is not to be seen.
As in the days of antient fame
Prophets and poets were the same,
And all the praise that poets gain
Is but for what th' invent and feign:
So gain'd our 'Squire his fame by seeing
Such things as never would have being.

Whence

Whence he for oracles was grown
The very tripod[11] of his town.
Gazettes no sooner rose a lye in,
But straight he fell to prophesying;
Made dreadful slaughter in his course,
O'erthrew provincials, foot and horse;
Brought armies o'er by sudden pressings
Of Hanoverians, Swiss and Hessians[15];
Feasted with blood his Scottish clan,
And hang'd all rebels, to a man;
Divided their estates and pelf,
And took a goodly share himself[16].
All this with spirit energetic,
He did by second-sight prophetic.

Thus stor'd with intellectual riches,
Skill'd was our 'Squire in making speeches,
Where strength of brain united centers
With strength of lungs surpassing Stentor's[17].
But as some musquets so contrive it,
As oft to miss the mark they drive at,
And tho' well aim'd at duck or plover,
Bear wide and kick their owners over:

So

So far'd our 'Squire, whose reas'ning toil
Would often on himself recoil,
And so much injur'd more his side,
The stronger arg'ments he applied:
As old war-elephants dismay'd,
Trode down the troops they came to aid,
And hurt their own side more in battle
Than less and ordinary cattle.[18]
Yet at town-meetings ev'ry chief
Pinn'd faith on great M'Fingal's sleeve,
And as he motion'd, all by rote
Rais'd sympathetic hands to vote.

The town, our Hero's scene of action,
Had long been torn by feuds of faction,
And as each party's strength prevails,
It turn'd up diff'rent, heads or tails;
With constant rattling in a trice
Show'd various sides as oft as dice:
As that fam'd weaver, wife t' Ulysses,
By night each day's work pick'd in pieces,
An tho' she stoutly did bestir her,
Its finishing was ne'er the nearer[19]:

So

So did this town with ftedfaft zeal
Weave cob-webs for the public weal,
Which when compleated, or before,
A fecond vote in pieces tore.
They met, made fpeeches full long winded,
Refolv'd, protefted, and refcinded;
Addreffes figned, then chofe Committees,
To ftop all drinking of Bohea-teas;
With winds of doctrine veer'd about,
And turn'd all Whig-Committees out[20].
Meanwhile our Hero, as their head,
In pomp the tory[21] faction led,
Still following, as the 'Squire fhould please,
Succeffive on, like files of geefe.

And now the town was fummon'd greeting,
To grand parading of town-meeting;
A fhow, that ftrangers might appall,
As Rome's grave fenate did the Gaul[22].
High o'er the rout, on pulpit ftairs[23],
Like den of thieves in houfe of pray'rs,
(That houfe, which loth a rule to break,
Serv'd heav'n but one day in the week,

Open

Open the reft for all fupplies
Of news and politics and lies)
Stood forth the conftable, and bore
His ftaff, like Merc'ry's wand of yore[24],
Wav'd potent round, the peace to keep,
As that laid dead men's fouls to fleep.
Above and near th' hermetic ftaff,
The moderator's upper half,
In grandeur o'er the cufhion bow'd,
Like Sol half-feen behind a cloud.[25]
Beneath ftood voters of all colours,
Whigs, tories, orators and bawlers,
With ev'ry tongue in either faction,
Prepar'd, like minute-men[26], for action;
Where truth and falfehood, wrong and right,
Draw all their legions out to fight;
With equal uproar, fcarcely rave,
Oppofing winds in Æolus' cave[27];
Such dialogues with earneft face,
Held never Balaam with his afs[28].

   With daring zeal and courage bleft
Honorius[29] firft the crowd addrefs'd;

                         When

When now our 'Squire returning late,
Arrived to aid the grand debate,
With ſtrange four faces ſat him down,
While thus the orator went on.

"— For ages bleſt, thus Britain roſe
The terror of encircling foes;
Her heroes rul'd the bloody plain;
Her conq'ring ſtandard aw'd the main:
The diff'rent palms her triumphs grace,
Of arms in war, of arts in peace:
Unharraſſ'd by maternal care,
Each riſing province flouriſh'd fair;
Whoſe various wealth with lib'ral hand,
By far o'er-paid the parent-land[30].
But tho' ſo bright her ſun might ſhine,
'Twas quickly haſting to decline,
With feeble rays, too weak t' aſſuage,
The damps, that chill the eve of age.

For ſtates, like men, are doom'd as well
Th' infirmities of age to feel[31];

And

And from their diff'rent forms of empire
Are seiz'd with ev'ry deep distemper.
Some states high fevers have made head in,
Which nought could cure but copious bleeding;
While others have grown dull and dozy,
Or fix'd in helpless idiocy;
Or turn'd demoniacs to belabour
Each peaceful habitant and neighbour;
Or vex't with hypocondriac fits,
Have broke their strength and lost their wits.

Thus now while hoary years prevail,
Good Mother Britain seem'd to fail;
Her back bent, crippled with the weight
Of age and debts and cares of state:
For debts she ow'd, and those so large,
As twice her wealth could not discharge,
And now 'twas thought, so high they'd grown,
She'd break and come upon the town[32];
Her arms, of nations once the dread,
She scarce could lift above her head;
Her deafen'd ears ('twas all their hope)
The final trump perhaps might ope,

So

So long they'd been in ftupid mood,
Shut to the hearing of all good;
Grim Death had put her in his fcroll,
Down on the execution-roll;
And Gallic crows, as fhe grew weaker,
Began to whet their beaks to pick her [33]
And now her pow'rs decaying faft,
Her grand Climact'ric had fhe paft,
And, juft like all old women elfe,
Fell in the vapours much by fpells.
Strange whimfies on her fancy ftruck,
And gave her brain a difmal fhock;
Her mem'ry fails, her judgment ends;
She quite forgot her neareft friends,
Loft all her former fenfe and knowledge,
And fitted faft for Beth'lem college [34];
Of all the pow'rs fhe once retain'd,
Conceit and pride alone remain'd.
As Eve when falling was fo modeft
To fancy fhe fhould grow a goddefs [35];
As madmen, ftraw who long have flept on,
Will ftile them, Jupiter or Neptune:

So

So Britain 'midſt her airs ſo flighty,
Now took a whim to be Almighty;
Urg'd on to deſp'rate heights of frenzy,
Affirm'd her own Omnipotency[36];
Would rather ruin all her race,
Than 'bate Supremacy an ace;
Aſſumed all rights divine, as grown
The churches head[37], like good Pope Joan[38];
Swore all the world ſhould bow and ſkip
To her almighty Goodyſhip;
Anath'matiz'd each unbeliever,
And vow'd to live and rule forever.
Her ſervants humour'd every whim,
And own'd at once her pow'r ſupreme,
Her follies pleas'd in all their ſtages,
For ſake of legacies and wages;
In Stephen's Chapel[39] then in ſtate too
Set up her golden calf to pray to,
Proclaim'd its pow'r and right divine,
And call'd for worſhip at its ſhrine,
And for poor Heretics to burn us,
Bade North[40] prepare his fiery furnace;

Struck

Struck bargains with the Romish churches
Infallibility to purchase;
Set wide for Popery the door,
Made friends with Babel's scarlet whore [41],
Join'd both the matrons firm in clan;
No sisters made a better span.
No wonder then, ere this was over,
That she should make her children suffer.
She first, without pretence of reason,
Claim'd right whate'er we had to seize on;
And with determin'd resolution,
To put her claims in execution,
Sent fire and sword, and called it, Lenity,
Starv'd us, and christen'd it, Humanity [42].
For she, her case grown desperater,
Mistook the plainest things in nature;
Had lost all use of eyes or wits;
Took slav'ry for the bill of rights [43];
Trembled at Whigs and deem'd them foes,
And stopp'd at loyalty her nose;
Stiled her own children, brats and caitiffs,
And knew us not from th' Indian natives.

        What

What tho' with supplicating pray'r
We begg'd our lives and goods she'd spare[44];
Not vainer vows, with sillier call,
Elijah's prophets rais'd to Baal[45];
A worshipp'd stock of god, or goddess,
Had better heard and understood us.
So once Egyptians at the Nile
Ador'd their guardian Crocodile,
Who heard them first with kindest ear,
And ate them to reward their pray'r[46];
And could he talk, as kings can do,
Had made as gracious speeches too[47].

Thus spite of pray'rs her schemes pursuing,
She still went on to work our ruin;
Annull'd our charters of releases[48],
And tore our title-deeds in pieces;
Then sign'd her warrants of ejection,
And gallows rais'd to stretch our necks on:
And on these errands sent in rage,
Her bailiff, and her hangman, Gage[49],
And at his heels, like dogs to bait us,
Dispatch'd her Posse Comitatus[50].

No state e'er chose a fitter person,
To carry such a silly farce on.
As Heathen gods in antient days
Received at second-hand their praise,
Stood imag'd forth in stones and stocks,
And deified in barber's blocks;
So Gage was chose to represent
Th' omnipotence of Parliament.
And as old heroes gain'd, by shifts,
From gods, as poets tell, their gifts;
Our Gen'ral, as his actions show,
Gain'd like assistance from below,
By Satan graced with full supplies,
From all his magazine of lies.
Yet could his practice ne'er impart
The wit to tell a lie with art.
Those lies alone are formidable,
Where artful truth is mixt with fable;
But Gage has bungled oft so vilely,
No soul would credit lies so silly,
Outwent all faith and stretch'd beyond
Credulity's extremest end.

Whence

Whence plain it seems tho' Satan once
O'erlook'd with scorn each brainless dunce,
And blund'ring brutes in Eden shunning,
Chose out the serpent for his cunning[51];
Of late he is not half so nice,
Nor picks assistants, 'cause they're wise.
For had he stood upon perfection,
His present friends had lost th' election,
And far'd as hard in this proceeding,
As owls and asses did in Eden.

Yet fools are often dang'rous enemies,
As meanest reptiles are most venomous;
Nor e'er could Gage by craft and prowess
Have done a whit more mischief to us:
Since he began th' unnatural war,
The work his masters sent him for.

And are there in this freeborn land
Among ourselves a venal band,
A dastard race, who long have sold
Their souls and consciences for gold;

Who wish to stab their country's vitals,
If they might heir surviving titles;
With joy behold our mischiefs brewing,
Insult and triumph in our ruin?
Priests who, if Satan should sit down,
To make a Bible of his own,
Would gladly for the sake of mitres,
Turn his inspir'd and sacred writers;
Lawyers, who should he wish to prove
His title t' his old seat above,
Would, if his cause he'd give 'em fees in,
Bring writs of Entry sur disseisin[52],
Plead for him boldly at the session,
And hope to put him in possession;
Merchants who, for his kindly aid,
Would make him partners in their trade,
Hang out their signs in goodly show,
Inscrib'd with 'Beelzebub and Co.'
And Judges, who would list his pages,
For proper liveries and wages;
And who as humbly cringe and bow
To all his mortal servants now?

There

There are; and shame with pointing gestures,
Marks out th' Addressers and Protesters [53];
Whom, following down the stream of fate,
Contempts ineffable await,
And public infamy forlorn,
Dread hate and everlasting scorn."

   As thus he spake, our 'Squire M'Fingal
Gave to his partizans a signal.
Not quicker roll'd the waves to land,
When Moses wav'd his potent wand,
Nor with more uproar, than the Tories
Set up a gen'ral rout in chorus;
Laugh'd, hifs'd, hem'd, murmur'd, groan'd and jeer'd;
Honorius now could scarce be heard.
Our Muse amid th' increasing roar,
Could not distinguish one word more:
Tho' she sat by, in firm record
To take in shorthand ev'ry word;
As antient Muses wont, to whom
Old Bards for depositions come;
Who must have writ 'em; for how else
Could they each speech verbatim tell 's?

                                    And

And tho' some readers of romances
Are apt to strain their tortur'd fancies,
And doubt, when lovers all alone
Their sad soliloquies do groan,
Grieve many a page with no one near 'em,
And nought but rocks and groves to hear 'em,
What spright infernal could have tattled,
And told the authors all they prattled;
Whence some weak minds have made objection,
That what they scribbled must be fiction:
'Tis false; for while the lovers spoke,
The Muse was by, with table-book,
And least some blunder might ensue,
Echo stood clerk and kept the cue.
And tho' the speech ben't worth a groat,
As usual, 'tisn't the author's fault,
But error merely of the prater,
Who should have talk'd to th' purpose better:
Which full excuse, my critic-brothers,
May help me out, as well as others;
And 'tis design'd, tho' here it lurk,
To serve as preface to this work.

So

So let it be—for now our 'Squire
No longer could contain his ire;
And rising 'midst applauding Tories,
Thus vented wrath upon Honorius.

Quoth he, "'Tis wondrous what strange stuff
Your Whig's-heads are compounded of;
Which force of logic cannot pierce,
Nor syllogistic carte & tierce,
Nor weight of scripture or of reason
Suffice to make the least impression.
Not heeding what ye rais'd contest on,
Ye prate, and beg or steal the question;
And when your boasted arguings fail,
Strait leave all reas'ning off, to rail.
Have not our High-Church Clergy[51] made it
Appear from scriptures which ye credit,
That right divine from heav'n was lent
To kings, that is the Parliament,
Their subjects to opprefs and teaze,
And serve the Devil when they please?
Did they not write and pray and preach,
And torture all the parts of speech,

About Rebellion make a pother,
From one end of the land to th' other?
And yet gain'd fewer prof'lyte Whigs,
Than old St. Anth'ny 'mongst the pigs;
And chang'd not half so many vicious
As Austin, when he preach'd to fishes;
Who throng'd to hear, the legend tells,
Were edified and wagg'd their tails [55]:
But scarce you'd prove it, if you tried,
That e'er one Whig was edified.
Have ye not heard from Parson Walter [56]
Much dire presage of many a halter?
What warnings had ye of your duty
From our old Rev'rend Sam. Auchmuty [57]?
From Priests of all degrees and metres,
T' our fag-end man poor Parson Peters [58]?
Have not our Cooper [59] and our Seabury [60]
Sung hymns, like Barak and old Deborah [61];
Prov'd all intrigues to set you free
Rebellion 'gainst the pow'rs that be;
Brought over many a scripture text
That us'd to wink at rebel sects,

Coax'd

Coax'd wayward ones to favour regents,
Or paraphras'd them to obedience;
Prov'd ev'ry king, ev'n those confest
Horns of th' Apocalyptic beast [62],
And sprouting from its noddles seven,
Ordain'd, as bishops are, by heav'n;
(For reasons sim'lar, as we're told
That Tophet was ordain'd of old)
By this lay-ordination valid
Becomes all sanctified and hallow'd,
Takes patent out when heav'n has sign'd it,
And starts up strait, the Lord's anointed?
Like extreme unction that can cleanse
Each penitent from deadly sins,
Make them run glib, when oil'd by Priest,
The heav'nly road, like wheels new greas'd,
Serve them, like shoeball [63], for defences
'Gainst wear and tear of consciences:
So king's anointment cleans betimes,
Like fuller's earth [64], all spots of crimes,
For future knav'ries gives commissions,
Like Papists sinning under licence [65].

For

For heav'n ordain'd the origin,
Divines declare, of pain and sin;
Prove such great good they both have done us,
Kind mercy 'twas they came upon us:
For without pain and sin and folly
Man ne'er were blest, or wise, or holy;
And we should thank the Lord, 'tis so,
As authors grave wrote long ago.
Now heav'n its issues never brings
Without the means, and these are kings;
And he, who blames when they announce ills,
Would counteract th' eternal counsels.
As when the Jews, a murm'ring race,
By constant grumblings fell from grace,
Heav'n taught them first to know their distance,
By famine, slav'ry and Philistines;
When these could no repentance bring,
In wrath it sent them last a king[63]:
So nineteen, 'tis believ'd, in twenty
Of modern kings for plagues are sent you;
Nor can your cavillers pretend,
But that they answer well their end.

'Tis

'Tis yours to yield to their command,
As rods in Providence's hand;
And if it means to fend you pain,
You turn your nofes up in vain;
Your only way's in peace to bear it,
And make neceffity a merit.
Hence fure perdition muft await
The man, who rifes 'gainft the ftate,
Who meets at once the damning fentence,
Without one loophole for repentance;
E'en tho' he 'gain the royal fee,
And rank among the pow'rs that be[67]:
For hell is theirs, the fcripture fhows,
Whoe'er the pow'rs that be oppofe,
And all thofe pow'rs (I am clear that 'tis fo)
Are damn'd for ever, ex officio.

   Thus far our Clergy; but 'tis true,
We lack'd not earthly reaf'ners too.
Had I the Poet's brazen lungs[68]
As found-board to his hundred tongues,
I could not half the fcriblers mufter
That fwarm'd round Rivington[69] in clufter;
                 Affemblies,

Assemblies, Councilmen, forsooth;
Brush[70], Cooper[71], Wilkins[72], Chandler[73], Booth[74].
Yet all their arguments and sap'ence,
You did not value at three halfpence.
Did not our Massachusettensis[75]
For your conviction strain his senses?
Scrawl ev'ry moment he could spare,
From cards and barbers and the fair;
Show, clear as sun in noonday heavens,
You did not feel a single grievance;
Demonstrate all your opposition
Sprung from the eggs of foul sedition;
Swear he had seen the nest she laid in,
And knew how long she had been sitting;
Could tell exact what strength of heat is
Requir'd to hatch her out Committees[76];
What shapes they take, and how much longer's
The space before they grow t' a Congress?
New whitewash'd Hutchinson[77] and varnish'd,
Our Gage, who'd got a little tarnish'd,
Made 'em new masks, in time no doubt,
For Hutchinson's was quite worn out;

And

And while he muddled all his head
You did not heed a word he said.
Did not our grave Judge Sewall[78] hit
The summit of news-paper wit?
Fill'd ev'ry leaf of ev'ry paper
Of Mills and Hicks[79] and mother Draper[80];
Drew proclamations, works of toil,
In true sublime of scarecrow style;
Wrote farces too, 'gainst Sons of Freedom[81],
All for your good, and none would read 'em;
Denounc'd damnation on their frenzy,
Who died in Whig-impenitency;
Affirm'd that heav'n would lend us aid,
As all our Tory-writers said,
And calculated so its kindness,
He told the moment when it join'd us."

"'Twas then belike, Honorius cried,
When you the public fast defied[82],
Refus'd to heav'n to raise a prayer,
Because you'd no connections there;
And since with rev'rent hearts and faces
To Governors you'd make addresses,

In them, who made you Tories, feeing
You lived and mov'd and had your being;
Your humble vows you would not breathe
To pow'rs you'd no acquaintance with."

" As for your fafts, replied our 'Squire,
What circumftance could fafts require;
We kept them not, but 'twas no crime;
We held them merely lofs of time.
For what advantage firm and lafting,
Pray did you ever get by fafting?
And what the gains that can arife
From vows and off'rings to the fkies?
Will heav'n reward with pofts and fees,
Or fend us Tea, as Confignees[53],
Give penfions, fal'ries, places, bribes,
Or chufe us judges, clerks, or fcribes?
Has it commiffions in its gift,
Or cafh, to ferve us at a lift?
Are acts of parliament there made,
To carry on the placeman's trade?
Or has it pafs'd a fingle bill
To let us plunder whom we will?

And

And look our list of placemen all over;
Did heav'n appoint our chief judge, Oliver[84],
Fill that high bench with ignoramus,
Or has it councils by mandamus[85]?
Who made that wit of water-gruel[86],
A Judge of Admiralty, Sewall?
And were they not mere earthly struggles,
That rais'd up Murray[87], say, and Ruggles[88]?
Did heav'n send down, our pains to med'cine,
That old simplicity of Edson[89],
Or by election pick out from us,
That Marshfield blund'rer Nat. Ray Thomas[90];
Or had it any hand in serving
A Loring[91], Pepp'rell[92], Browne[93], or Erving[94]?

Yet we've some saints, the very thing,
We'll pit against the best you'll bring
For can the strongest fancy paint
Than Hutchinson a greater saint?
Was there a parson used to pray
At times more reg'lar twice a day;
As folks exact have dinners got,
Whether they've appetites or not?

Was there a zealot more alarming
'Gainſt public vice to hold forth ſermon,
Or fix'd at church, whoſe inward motion
Roll'd up his eyes with more devotion?
What Puritan[95] could ever pray
In Godlier tone, than treaſ'rer Gray[96],
Or at town-meetings ſpeechify'ng,
Could utter more melodious whine,
And ſhut his eyes and vent his moan,
Like owl afflicted in the ſun?
Who once ſent home his canting rival,
Lord Dartmouth's[97] ſelf, might outbedrivel."

"Have you forgot, Honorius cried,
How your prime ſaint the truth defied,
Affirm'd he never wrote a line
Your charter'd rights to undermine;
When his own letters then were by,
That prov'd his meſſage all a lie[98]?
How many promiſes he ſeal'd,
To get th' oppreſſive acts repeal'd,
Yet once arriv'd on England's ſhore,
Set on the Premier to paſs more[99]?

But

But these are no defects, we grant,
In a right loyal Tory faint,
Whose godlike virtues must with ease
Atone such venal crimes as these:
Or ye perhaps in scripture spy
A new commandment, 'Thou shalt lie;'
And if 't be so (as who can tell?)
There's no one sure ye keep so well."

" Quoth he, For lies and promise-breaking
Ye need not be in such a taking;
For lying is, we know and teach,
The highest privilege of speech;
The universal Magna Charta,
To which all human race is party,
Whence children first, as David says,
Lay claim to 't in their earliest days;
The only stratagem in war,
Our Gen'rals have occasion for;
The only freedom of the press
Our politicians need in peace:
And 'tis a shame you wish t' abridge us
Of these our darling privileges.

Thank

Thank heav'n, your shot have miss'd their aim,
For lying is no sin, or shame.

As men last wills may change again,
Tho' drawn in name of God, amen;
Besure they must have much the more,
O'er promises as great a pow'r,
Which made in haste, with small inspection,
So much the more will need correction;
And when they've careless spoke, or penn'd em,
Have right to look 'em o'er and mend 'em;
Revise their vows, or change the text,
By way of codicil annex'd,
Turn out a promise, that was base,
And put a better in its place.
So Gage of late agreed, you know,
To let the Boston people go;
Yet when he saw 'gainst troops that brav'd him,
They were the only guards that sav'd him [100],
Kept off that Satan of a Putnam,
From breaking in to maul and mutt'n him [101];
He'd too much wit such leagues t' observe,
And shut them in again to starve.

So

So Moses writes, when female Jews
Made oaths and vows unfit for use,
Their parents then might set them free
From that conscientious tyranny[102]:
And shall men feel that spir'tual bondage
Forever, when they grow beyond age;
Nor have pow'r their own oaths to change?
I think the tale were very strange.
Shall vows but bind the stout and strong,
And let go women weak and young,
As nets enclose the larger crew,
And let the smaller fry creep thro'?
Besides, the Whigs have all been set on,
The Tories to affright and threaten,
Till Gage amidst his trembling fits
Has hardly kept him in his wits;
And tho' he speak with art and finesse,
'Tis said beneath duress per minas.
For we're in peril of our souls
From feathers, tar and lib'rty-poles[103]:
And vows extorted are not binding
In law, and so not worth the minding.

For we have in this hurly-burly
Sent off our consciences on furlow,
Thrown our religion o'er in form;
Our ship to lighten in the storm.
Nor need we blush your Whigs before;
If we've no virtue you've no more.

Yet black with sins, would stain a mitre,
Rail ye at crimes by ten tints whiter,
And stuff'd with choler atrabilious,
Insult us here for peccadilloes?
While all your vices run so high
That mercy scarce could find supply:
While should you offer to repent,
You'd need more fasting days than Lent,
More groans than haunted churchyard vallies,
And more confessions than broad-alleys [14].
I'll show you all at fitter time,
The extent and greatness of your crime,
And here demonstrate to your face,
Your want of virtue, as of grace,
Evinced from topics old and recent:
But thus much must suffice at present.

To th' after-portion of the day,
I leave what more remains to say;
When I've good hope you'll all appear,
More fitted and prepared to hear,
And griev'd for all your vile demeanour
But now 'tis time t' adjourn for dinner."

M'FINGAL:

CANTO SECOND,

OR

The TOWN-MEETING, P. M.

THE Sun, who never stops to dine,
Two hours had pass'd the midway line,
And driving at his usual rate,
Lash'd on his downward car of state.
And now expired the short vacation,
And dinner done in epic fashion;
While all the crew beneath the trees,
Eat pocket-pies, or bread and cheese;
Nor shall we, like old Homer care
To versify their bill of fare.
For now each party, feasted well,
Throng'd in, like sheep, at sound of bell,

With

With equal spirit took their places;
And meeting oped with three Oh yesses':
When first the daring Whigs 't oppose,
Again the great M'Fingal rose,
Stretch'd magisterial arm amain,
And thus assum'd th' accusing strain.

" Ye Whigs attend, and hear affrighted
The crimes whereof ye stand indicted,
The sins and follies past all compass,
That prove you guilty or non compos.
I leave the verdict to your senses,
And jury of your consciences;
Which tho' they're neither good nor true,
Must yet convict you and your crew.
Ungrateful sons! a factious band,
That rise against your parent-land!
Ye viper'd race, that burst in strife,
The welcome womb, that gave you life,
Tear with sharp fangs and forked tongue,
Th' indulgent bowels, whence you sprung;
And scorn the debt of obligation
You justly owe the British nation,

Which

Which since you cannot pay, your crew
Affect to swear 'twas never due.
Did not the deeds of England's Primate [2]
First drive your fathers to this climate,
Whom jails and fines and ev'ry ill
Forc'd to their good against their will?
Ye owe to their obliging temper
The peopling your newfangled empire,
While ev'ry British act and canon
Stood forth your causa sine qua non.
Did they not send you charters o'er [3],
And give you lands you own'd before,
Permit you all to spill your blood,
And drive out heathen where you could;
On these mild terms, that conquest won,
The realm you gain'd should be their own.
Or when of late attack'd by those,
Whom her connection made your foes [4],
Did they not then, distrest in war,
Send Gen'rals to your help from far [5],
Whose aid you own'd in terms less haughty
And thankfully o'erpaid your quota? [6]

Say

Say, at what period did they grudge
To send you Governor or Judge,
With all their miffionary crew,
To teach you law and gofpel too?
Brought o'er all felons in the nation,
To help you on in population;
Propos'd their Bifhops to furrender,
And made their Priefts a legal tender,
Who only afk'd in furplice clad,
The fimple tythe of all you had⁷:
And now to keep all knaves in awe,
Have fent their troops t' eftablifh law,
And with gunpowder, fire and ball,
Reform your people one and all.
Yet when their infolence and pride
Have anger'd all the world befide,
When fear and want at once invade,
Can you refufe to lend them aid;
And rather rifque your heads in fight,
Than gratefully throw in your mite⁸?
Can they for debts make fatisfaction,
Should they difpofe their realm by auction;

And

And fell off Britain's goods and land all
To France and Spain by inch of candle?
Shall good king George, with want oppreft,
Infert his name in bankrupt lift,
And fhut up fhop, like failing merchant,
That fears the bailiffs fhould make fearch in't;
With poverty fhall princes ftrive,
And nobles lack whereon to live?
Have they not rack'd their whole inventions,
To feed their brats on pofts and penfions⁹,
Made ev'n Scotch friends with taxes groan,
And pick'd poor Ireland to the bone;
Yet have on hand as well deferving,
Ten thousand baftards left for ftarving?
And can you now with confcience clear,
Refufe them an afylum here,
Or not maintain in manner fitting
These genuine fons of mother Britain ¹⁰?
T' evade thefe crimes of blackeft grain,
You prate of liberty in vain,
And ftrive to hide your vile defigns,
With terms abftrufe like fchool-divines.

         Your

Your boasted patriotism is scarce,
And country's love is but a farce;
And after all the proofs you bring,
We Tories know there's no such thing.
Our English writers of great fame
Prove public virtue but a name.
Hath not Dalrymple [11] show'd in print,
And Johnson [12] too, there's nothing in't?
Produc'd you demonstration ample
From other's and their own example,
That self is still, in either faction,
The only principle of action;
The loadstone, whose attracting tether
Keeps the politic world together:
And spite of all your double-dealing,
We Tories know 'tis so, by feeling.

Who heeds your babbling of transmitting
Freedom to brats of your begetting,
Or will proceed as though there were a tie,
Or obligation to posterity [13]?
We get 'em, bear 'em, breed and nurse;
What has poster'ty done for us,

That

That we, left they their rights should lose,
Should trust our necks to gripe of noose?

And who believes you will not run?
You're cowards, ev'ry mother's son;
And should you offer to deny,
We've witnesses to prove it by.
Attend th' opinion first, as referee,
Of your old Gen'ral, stout Sir Jeffery [14],
Who swore that with five thousand foot
He'd rout you all, and in pursuit,
Run thro' the land as easily,
As camel thro' a needle's eye [15].
Did not the valiant Col'nel Grant
Against your courage make his slant,
Affirm your universal failure
In ev'ry principle of valour,
And swear no scamp'rers e'er could match you,
So swift, a bullet scarce could catch you [16]?
And will ye not confess in this,
A judge most competent he is,
Well skill'd on runnings to decide,
As what himself has often tried?

       'Twould

'Twould not methinks be labour lost,
If you'd sit down and count the cost;
And ere you call your Yankies out,
First think what work you've set about.
Have ye not rouz'd, his force to try on,
That grim old beast, the British lion?
And know you not that at a sup
He's large enough to eat you up?
Have you survey'd his jaws beneath,
Drawn inventories of his teeth,
Or have you weigh'd in even balance,
His strength and magnitude of talons?
His roar would turn your boasts to fear,
As easily as sour small-beer[17],
And make your feet from dreadful fray,
By native instinct run away.
Britain, depend on't will take on her
T' assert her dignity and honor,
And ere she'd lose your share of pelf,
Destroy your country and herself.
For has not North declar'd they fight
To gain substantial rev'nue by't[18],

Denied

Denied he'd ever deign to treat,
Till on your knees and at his feet?
And feel you not a trifling ague,
From Van's Delenda eft Carthago[19]?
For this, now Britain has come to't,
Think you fhe has not means to do't?
Has fhe not fet to work all engines
To fpirit up the native Indians,
Send on your backs a favage band,
With each a hatchet in his hand,
T' amufe themfelves with fcalping knives,
And butcher children and your wives[20];
That fhe may boaft again with vanity,
Her Englifh national humanity?
(For now in its primæval fenfe,
This term, human'ty, comprehends
All things of which, on this fide hell,
The human mind is capable;
And thus 'tis well, by writers fage,
Applied to Britain and to Gage.)
And on this work to raife allies,
She fent her duplicate of Guys,

To drive, at diff'rent parts at once, on
Her stout Guy Carlton and Guy Johnson[21];
To each of whom, to send again ye
Old Guy of Warwick were a ninny[22].
Tho' the dun cow he fell'd in war,
These killcows are his betters far[23].

   And has she not assay'd her notes,
To rouze your slaves to cut your throats,
Sent o'er ambassadors with guineas,
To bribe your blacks in Carolinas[24]?
And has not Gage, her missionary
Turn'd many an Afric slave t' a Tory,
And made th' Amer'can bishop's see grow,
By many a new-converted Negro[25]?
As friends to gov'rnment did not he
Their slaves at Boston late set free;
Enlist them all in black parade,
Set off with regimental red[26]?
And were they not accounted then
Among his very bravest men?
And when such means she stoops to take,
Think you she is not wide awake?

As Eliphaz' good man in Job
Own'd num'rous allies thro' the globe;
Had brought the ſtones along the ſtreet
To ratify a cov'nant meet,
And ev'ry beaſt from lice to lions,
To join in leagues of ſtrict alliance[27]:
Has ſhe not cring'd, in ſpite of pride,
For like aſſiſtance far and wide?
Was there a creature ſo deſpiſ'd,
Its aid ſhe has not ſought and priz'd?
Till all this formidable league roſe
Of Indians, Britiſh troops and Negroes[28],
And can you break theſe triple bands
By all your workmanſhip of hands?"

"Sir, quoth Honorius, we preſume
You gueſs from paſt feats, what's to come,
And from the mighty deeds of Gage,
Foretell how fierce the war he'll wage.
You doubtleſs recollected here
The annals of his firſt great year:
While wearying out the Tories' patience,
He ſpent his breath in proclamations;

While

While all his mighty noise and vapour
Was used in wrangling upon paper;
And boasted military fits
Closed in the straining of his wits;
While troops in Boston commons plac'd [29]
Laid nought but quires of paper waste;
While strokes alternate stunn'd the nation,
Protest, address and proclamation;
And speech met speech, fib clash'd with fib,
And Gage still answer'd, squib for squib.

Tho' this not all his time was lost on;
He fortified the town of Boston;
Built breastworks that might lend assistance
To keep the patriots at a distance [30];
(For howsoe'er the rogues might scoff,
He liked them best the farthest off)
Of mighty use and help to aid
His courage, when he felt afraid;
And whence right off in manful station,
He'd boldly pop his proclamation.
Our hearts must in our bosoms freeze
At such heroic deeds as these."

"Vain

"Vain," quoth the 'Squire, "you'll find to sneer
At Gage's first triumphant year;
For Providence, dispos'd to teaze us,
Can use what instruments it pleases.
To pay a tax at Peter's wish,
His chief cashier was once a Fish[31];
An Ass, in Balaam's sad disaster,
Turn'd orator and sav'd his master[32];
A Goose plac'd centry on his station
Preserv'd old Rome from desolation[33];
An English Bishop's Cur of late
Disclosed rebellions 'gainst the state[34];
So Frogs croak'd Pharaoh to repentance,
And Lice revers'd the threat'ning sentence[35]:
And heav'n can ruin you at pleasure,
By our scorn'd Gage, as well as Cæsar.
Yet did our hero in these days
Pick up some laurel wreaths of praise.
And as the statuary of Seville
Made his crackt saint an exc'llent devil;
So tho' our war few triumphs brings,
We gain'd great fame in other things.

Did

Did not our troops show much discerning,
And skill your various arts in learning?
Outwent they not each native Noodle[36]
By far in playing Yanky-doodle;
Which, as 'twas your New-England tune,
'Twas marvellous they took so soon[37]?
And ere the year was fully thro',
Did not they learn to foot it too;
And such a dance as ne'er was known,
For twenty miles on end lead down?
Was there a Yanky trick you knew,
They did not play as well as you?
Did they not lay their heads together,
And gain your art to tar and feather,
When Col'nel Nesbitt thro' the town,
In triumph bore the country-clown?
Oh, what a glorious work to sing
The vet'ran troops of Britain's king,
Advent'ring for th' heroic laurel,
With bag of feathers and tar-barrel!
To paint the cart where culprits ride,
And Nesbitt marching at its side,

Great executioner and proud,
Like hangman high on Holbourn road;
And o'er the bright triumphal car
The waving enfigns of the war[38]!
As when a triumph Rome decreed,
For great Calig'la's valiant deed,
Who had fubdued the Britifh feas,
By gath'ring cockles from their bafe[39];
In pompous car the conqu'ror bore
His captiv'd fcallops from the fhore,
Ovations gain'd his crabs for fetching,
And mighty feats of oyfter-catching·
O'er Yankies thus the war begun,
They tarr'd and triumph'd over one .
And fought and boafted thro' the feafon,
With might as great, and equal reafon.

Yet thus, tho' fkill'd in vict'ry's toils,
They boaft, not unexpert, in wiles.
For gain'd they not an equal fame in
The arts of fecrecy and fcheming?
In ftratagems fhow'd mighty force,
And moderniz'd the Trojan horfe,

Play'd

Play'd o'er again thofe tricks Ulyffean,
In their fam'd Salem-expedition?
For as that horfe, the Poets tell ye,
Bore Grecian armies in his belly;
Till their full reck'ning run, with joy
Their Sinon midwif'd them in Troy[40]:
So in one fhip was Leslie[41] bold
Cramm'd with three hundred men in hold,
Equipp'd for enterprize and fail,
Like Jonas ftow'd in womb of whale.
To Marblehead[42] in depth of night,
The cautious veffel wing'd her flight.
And now the fabbath's filent day
Call'd all your Yankies off to pray;
Remov'd each prying jealous neighbour,
The fcheme and veffel fell in labour;
Forth from its hollow womb pour'd haft'ly
The Myrmidons of Col'nel Leflie:
Not thicker o'er the blacken'd ftrand
The frogs' detachment rufh'd to land,
Equipp'd by onfet or furprize
To ftorm th' entrenchment of the mice[43].

Thro'

Thro' Salem ſtrait without delay,
The bold battalion took its way,
March'd o'er a bridge in open ſight
Of ſev'ral Yankies arm'd for fight,
Then without loſs of time, or men
Veer'd round for Boſton back again;
And found ſo well their projects thrive,
That ev'ry ſoul got home alive [44].

Thus Gage's arms did fortune bleſs
With triumph, ſafety and ſuccess:
But mercy is without diſpute
His firſt and darling attribute;
So great it far outwent and conquer'd
His military ſkill at Concord [45].
There when the war he choſe to wage
Shone the benevolence of Gage;
Sent troops to that ill-omen'd place
On errands meer of ſpecial grace,
And all the work he choſe them for
Was to prevent a civil war [46]:
And for that purpoſe he projected
The only certain way t' effect it,

To

To take your powder, stores and arms,
And all your means of doing harms:
As prudent folks take knives away,
Left children cut themselves at play.
And yet tho' this was all his scheme,
This war you still will charge on him;
And tho' he oft has swore and said it,
Stick close to facts and give no credit.
Think you, he wish'd you'd brave and beard him?
Why, 'twas the very thing that fear'd him.
He'd rather you should all have run,
Than stay'd to fire a single gun.
And for the civil war you lament,
Faith, you yourselves must take the blame in't;
For had you then, as he intended,
Giv'n up your arms, it must have ended.
Since that's no war, each mortal knows,
Where one side only gives the blows,
And th' other bears 'em; on reflection
The most you'll call it is correction.
Nor could the contest have gone higher,
If you had ne'er return'd the fire;

But

But when you shot, and not before,
It then commenc'd a civil war[47].
Else Gage, to end this controversy,
Had but corrected you in mercy:
Whom mother Britain old and wise,
Sent o'er, the Col'nies to chastise;
Command obedience on their peril
Of ministerial whip and ferule;
And since they ne'er must come of age,
Govern'd and tutor'd them by Gage.
Still more, that this was all their errand,
The army's conduct makes apparent.
What tho' at Lexington you can say
They kill'd a few they did not fancy,
At Concord then, with manful popping,
Discharg'd a round the ball to open?
Yet when they saw your rebel-rout
Determin'd still to hold it out;
Did they not show their love to peace,
And wish, that discord strait might cease,
Demonstrate, and by proofs uncommon,
Their orders were to injure no man?

For

For did not ev'ry Reg'lar run
As foon as e'er you fir'd a gun[48];
Take the first fhot you fent them greeting,
As meant their fignal for retreating;
And fearful if they ftaid for fport,
You might by accident be hurt,
Convey themfelves with fpeed away
Full twenty miles in half a day[49];
Race till their legs were grown fo weary,
They'd fcarce fuffice their weight to carry?
Whence Gage extols, from gen'ral hearfay,
The great activ'ty of Lord Piercy[50];
Whofe brave example led them on,
And fpirited the troops to run;
And now may boaft at royal levees
A Yanky-chafe worth forty Chevys[51].
Yet you as vile as they were kind,
Purfued, like tygers, ftill behind,
Fir'd on them at your will, and fhut
The town, as tho' you'd ftarve them out;
And with parade prepoft'rous hedg'd
Affect to hold them there befieg'd[52];

(Tho'

('Tho' Gage, whom proclamations call
Your Gov'rnor and Vice-Admiral,
Whose pow'r gubernatorial still
Extends as far as Bunker's hill;
Whose admiralty reaches clever,
Near half a mile up Myftic river[53],
Whose naval force commands the seas,
Can run away when'er he please)
Scar'd troops of Tories into town,
And burnt their hay and houses down,
And menac'd Gage, unless he'd flee,
To drive him headlong to the sea[54];
As once, to faithless Jews a sign,
The de'el, turn'd hog-reeve, did the swine[55].

But now your triumphs all are o'er;
For see from Britain's angry shore
With mighty hosts of valour join
Her Howe, her Clinton and Burgoyne[56].
As comets thro' the affrighted skies
Pour baleful ruin, as they rife[57];
As Ætna with infernal roar
In conflagration sweeps the shore;

Or

Or as Abijah White when sent
Our Marshfield friends to represent,
Himself while dread array involves,
Commissions, pistols, swords, resolves,
In awful pomp descending down,
Bore terror on the factious town [58]:
Not with less glory and affright,
Parade these Gen'rals forth to fight.
No more each Reg'lar Col'nel runs
From whizzing beetles, as air-guns,
Thinks hornbugs bullets, or thro' fears
Muskitoes takes for musketeers;
Nor 'scapes, as tho' you'd gain'd allies
From Belzebub's whole host of flies.
No bug their warlike hearts appalls;
They better know the sound of balls [59].
I hear the din of battle bray,
The trump of horror marks its way.
I see afar the sack of cities,
The gallows strung with Whig-committees [60];
Your Moderators triced, like vermin,
And gate-posts graced with heads of Chairmen;

Your Gen'rals for wave-off'rings hanging⁶¹,
And ladders throng'd with Priests haranguing.
What pill'ries glad the Tories' eyes
With patriot-ears for sacrifice!
What whipping-posts your chosen race
Admit succeffive in embrace⁶²,
While each bears off his crimes, alack!
Like Bunyan's pilgrim, on his back⁶³;
Where then, when Tories scarce get clear,
Shall Whigs and Congresses appear?
What rocks and mountains shall you call
To wrap you over with their fall,
And save your heads in these sad weathers,
From fire and sword, and tar and feathers!
For lo, with British troops tarbright,
Again our Nesbitt heaves in sight!
He comes, he comes, your lines to storm,
And rig your troops in uniform⁶⁴!
To meet such heroes, will ye brag,
With fury arm'd, and feather-bag;
Who wield their missile pitch and tar,
With engines new in British war?

Lo, where our mighty navy brings
Deftruction on her canvas-wings[65],
While thro' the deeps her potent thunder,
Shall found th' alarm to rob and plunder!
As Phœbus firft, fo Homer fpeaks,
When he march'd out t' attack the Greeks[66],
'Gainft mules fent forth his arrows fatal,
And flew th' auxiliaries, their cattle;
So where our fhips fhall ftretch the keel,
What conquer'd oxen fhall they fteal!
What heroes rifing from the deep
Invade your marfhall'd hofts of fheep!
Difperfe whole troops of horfe, and preffing,
Make cows furrender at difcretion;
Attack your hens, like Alexanders,
And reg'ments rout of geefe and ganders;
Or where united arms combine
Lead captive many a herd of fwine[67]!
Then rufh in dreadful fury down
To fire on ev'ry feaport town;
Difplay their glory and their wits,
Fright unarm'd children into fits,

       And

And stoutly from th' unequal fray,
Make many a woman run away[68]!
And can ye doubt whene'er we please
Our chiefs shall boast such deeds as these?
Have we not chiefs transcending far,
The old fam'd thunderbolts of war;
Beyond the brave romantic fighters,
Stiled swords of death by novel-writers?
Nor in romancing ages e'er rose
So terrible a tier of heroes.
From Gage, what flashes fright the waves!
How loud a blunderbuss is Graves[69]!
How Newport dreads the blustring sallies,
That thunder from our popgun, Wallace,
While noise in formidable strains
Spouts from his thimble-full of brains[70]!
I see you sink with aw'd surprize!
I see our Tory-brethren rise!
And as the sect'ries Sandemanian,
Our friends describe their wish'd Millennium[71];
Tell how the world in ev'ry region
At once shall own their true religion;

For

For heav'n with plagues of awful dread,
Shall knock all heretics o' th' head;
And then their church, the meek in spirit,
The earth, as promis'd, shall inherit,
From the dead wicked, as heirs male,
And next remainder-men in tail:
Such ruin shall the Whigs oppress!
Such spoils our Tory friends shall bless!
While Confiscation at command[12]
Shall stalk in horror thro' the land,
Shall give your Whig-estates away,
And call our brethren into play.

And can ye doubt or scruple more,
These things are near you at the door?
Behold! for tho' to reas'ning blind,
Signs of the times ye sure might mind,
And view impending fate as plain
As ye'd foretell a show'r of rain.

Hath not heav'n warn'd you what must ensue,
And Providence declar'd against you;

Hung

Hung forth its dire portents of war,
By signs and beacons in the air [73];
Alarm'd old women all around
By fearful noises under ground;
While earth for many dozen leagues
Groan'd with her dismal load of Whigs?
Was there a meteor far and wide
But muster'd on the Tory-side?
A star malign that has not bent
Its aspects for the Parliament,
Foreboding your defeat and misery;
As once they fought against old Sisera [74]?
Was there a cloud that spread the skies,
But bore our armies of allies?
While dreadful hosts of fire stood forth
'Mid baleful glimm'rings from the North;
Which plainly shows which part they join'd,
For North's the minister, ye mind;
Whence oft your quibblers in gazettes
On Northern blasts have strain'd their wits [75];
And think ye not the clouds know how
To make the pun as well as you?

Did

Did there arife an apparition,
But grinn'd forth ruin to fedition?
A death-watch, but has join'd our leagues,
And click'd deftruction to the Whigs?
Heard ye not, when the wind was fair,
At night our or'tors in the air,
That, loud as admiralty-libel,
Read awful chapters from the bible,
And death and deviltry denounc'd,
And told you how you'd foon be trounc'd?
I fee to join our conqu'ring fide
Heav'n, earth and hell at once allied!
See from your overthrow and end
The Tories paradife afcend;
Like that new world that claims its ftation
Beyond the final conflagration!
I fee the day that lots your fhare
In utter darknefs and defpair;
The day of joy, when North, our Lord,
His faithful fav'rites fhall reward!
No Tory then fhall fet before him
Small wifh of 'Squire, or Juftice Quorum;

But

But 'fore his unmistaken eyes
See Lordships, posts and pensions rise.
Awake to gladness then, ye Tories,
Th' unbounded prospect lies before us?
The pow'r display'd in Gage's banners
Shall cut Amer'can lands to manors,
And o'er our happy conquer'd ground
Dispense estates and titles round.
Behold, the world shall stare at new setts
Of home-made earls in Massachusetts [76];
Admire, array'd in ducal tassels,
Your Ol'vers, Hutchinsons and Vassals [77];
See join'd in ministerial work
His grace of Albany and York [78]!
What Lordships from each carv'd estate,
On our New-York Assembly wait!
What titled Jauncys [79], Gales [80] and Billops [81];
Lord Brush [82], Lord Wilkins [83] and Lord Philips [84]!
In wide-sleev'd pomp of godly guise,
What solemn rows of bishops rise!
Aloft a card'nal's hat is spread
O'er punster Cooper's [85] rev'rend head!

In

In Vardell[86], that poetic zealot,
I view a lawn-bedizen'd prelate!
While mitres fall, as 'tis their duty,
On heads of Chandler and Auchmuty[87]!
Knights, viscounts, barons shall ye meet
As thick as pavements in the street!
Ev'n I perhaps, heav'n speed my claim,
Shall fix a Sir before my name.
For titles all our foreheads ache;
For what blest changes can they make!
Place rev'rence, grace and excellence
Where neither claim'd the least pretence;
Transform by patent's magic words
Men, likest devils, into Lords;
Whence commoners to peers translated
Are justly said to be created[88]!
Now where commissioners ye saw
Shall boards of nobles deal you law!
Long-robed comptrollers judge your rights,
And tide-waiters start up in knights!
While Whigs subdued in slavish awe,
Our wood shall hew, our water draw,

And

And bless that mildness, when past hope,
Which sav'd their necks from noose of rope.
For as to gain assistance we
Design their Negroes to set free;
For Whigs, when we enough shall bang 'em,
Perhaps 'tis better not to hang 'em;
Except their chiefs; the vulgar knaves
Will do more good preserv'd for slaves."

" 'Tis well, Honorius cried, your scheme
Has painted out a pretty dream.
We can't confute your second sight;
We shall be slaves and you a knight:
These things must come; but I divine
They'll come not in your day, or mine.
But oh, my friends, my brethren, hear,
And turn for once th' attentive ear.
Ye see how prompt to aid our woes,
The tender mercies of our foes;
Ye see with what unvaried rancour
Still for our blood their minions hanker,
Nor aught can sate their mad ambition,
From us, but death, or worse, submission.

Shall thefe then riot in our fpoil,
Reap the glad harveſt of our toil,
Rife from their country's ruin proud,
And roll their chariot wheels in blood?
And can ye fleep while high outfpread
Hangs defolation o'er your head?
See Gage with inaufpicious ſtar
Has oped the gates of civil war;
When ſtreams of gore from freemen ſlain,
Encrimfon'd Concord's fatal plain;
Whofe warning voice with awful found,
Still cries, like Abel's from the ground,
And heav'n, attentive to its call,
Shall doom the proud oppreffor's fall[89].

Rife then, ere ruin fwift furprize,
To victory, to vengeance rife!
Hark, how the diſtant din alarms!
The echoing trumpet breathes, to arms;
From provinces remote, afar,
The fons of glory rouze to war;
'Tis freedom calls; th' enraptur'd found
The Apalachian hills rebound[90];

The

The Georgian shores her voice shall hear[91],
And start from lethargies of fear.
From the parch'd zone, with glowing ray,
Where pours the sun intenser day,
To shores where icy waters roll,
And tremble to the dusky pole,
Inspir'd by freedom's heav'nly charms,
United nations wake to arms.
The star of conquest lights their way,
And guides their vengeance on their prey—
Yes, tho' tyrannic force oppose,
Still shall they triumph o'er their foes,
Till heav'n the happy land shall bless,
With safety, liberty and peace.

And ye whose souls of dastard mould
Start at the brav'ry of the bold;
To love your country who pretend,
Yet want all spirit to defend;
Who feel your fancies so prolific,
Engend'ring vision'd whims terrific,
O'er-run with horrors of coercion,
Fire, blood and thunder in reversion,

King's

King's standards, pill'ries, confiscations,
And Gage's scarecrow proclamations[97],
With all the trumpery of fear;
Hear bullets whizzing in your rear;
Who scarce could rouze, if caught in fray,
Presence of mind to run away;
See nought but halters rise to view
In all your dreams (and dreams are true);
And while these phantoms haunt your brains,
Bow down the willing neck to chains;
Heav'ns! are ye sons of sires so great,
Immortal in the fields of fate,
Who brav'd all deaths by land or sea,
Who bled, who conquer'd to be free!
Hence, coward souls, the worst disgrace
Of our forefathers' valiant race;
Hie homeward from the glorious field;
There turn the wheel, the distaff wield;
Act what ye are, nor dare to stain
The warrior's arms with touch profane:
There beg your more heroic wives
To guard your children and your lives;

Beneath

Beneath their aprons find a screen,
Nor dare to mingle more with men."

As thus he said, the Tories' anger
Could now restrain itself no longer,
Who tried before by many a freak, or
Insulting noise, to stop the speaker;
Swung th' unoil'd hinge of each pew-door;
Their feet kept shuffling on the floor;
Made their disapprobation known
By many a murmur, hum and groan,
That to his speech supplied the place
Of counterpart in thorough-base:
As bag-pipes, while the tune they breathe,
Still drone and grumble underneath;
Or as the fam'd Demosthenes
Harangued the rumbling of the seas,
Held forth with eloquence full grave
To audience loud of wind and wave[93];
And had a stiller congregation
Than Tories are to hear th' oration.
But now the storm grew high and louder
As nearer thunderings of a cloud are,

And

And ev'ry foul with heart and voice
Supplied his quota of the noise;
Each liftening ear was fet on torture
Each Tory bell'wing out, to order;
And fome, with tongue not low or weak,
Were clam'ring faft, for leave to fpeak;
The moderator, with great vi'lence,
The cufhion thump'd with "Silence, filence;"
The conftable to ev'ry prater
Bawl'd out, "Pray hear the moderator[94];"
Some call'd the vote, and fome in turn
Were fcreaming high, "Adjourn, adjourn:"
Not chaos heard fuch jars and clafhes
When all the el'ments fought for places.
Each bludgeon foon for blows was tim'd;
Each fift ftood ready cock'd and prim'd;
The ftorm each moment louder grew;
His fword the great M'Fingal drew,
Prepar'd in either chance to fhare,
To keep the peace, or aid the war.
Nor lack'd they each poetic being,
Whom bards alone are fkill'd in feeing;

Plum'd

Plum'd Victory ſtood perch'd on high,
Upon the pulpit-canopy [95].
To join, as is her cuſtom tried,
Like Indians, on the ſtrongeſt ſide;
The Deſtinies with ſhears and diſtaff,
Drew near their threads of life to twiſt off [96];
The Furies 'gan to feaſt on blows [97],
And broken heads or bloody noſe;
When on a ſudden from without
Aroſe a loud terrific ſhout;
And ſtrait the people all at once heard
Of tongues an univerſal concert:
Like Æſop's times, as fable runs,
When ev'ry creature talk'd at once [98],
Or like the variegated gabble
That craz'd the carpenters of Babel [99].
Each party ſoon forgot the quarrel,
And let the other go on parole;
Eager to know what fearful matter
Had conjur'd up ſuch gen'ral clatter;
And left the church in thin array,
As tho' it had been lecture-day [100].

Our 'Squire M'Fingal ſtraitway beckon'd
The conſtable to ſtand his ſecond,
And ſallied forth with afpect fierce
The crowd aſſembled to diſperſe.
The moderator out of view
Beneath a bench had lain perdue;
Peep'd up his head to view the fray,
Beheld the wranglers run away,
And left alone with ſolemn face,
Adjourn'd them without time or place.

END OF CANTO SECOND.

M‘FINGAL:

CANTO THIRD,

OR

THE LIBERTY POLE.

NOW arm'd with minifterial ire,
 Fierce fallied forth our loyal 'Squire,
And on his ftriding fteps attends,
His defp'rate clan of Tory friends;
When fudden met his angry eye,
A pole afcending thro' the fky,
Which num'rous throngs of Whiggifh race
Were raifing in the market-place¹;
Not higher fchool-boys kites afpire,
Or royal maft or country fpire,
Like fpears at Brobdignagian tilting²,
Or Satan's walking-ftaff in Milton³;

And

And on its top the flag unfurl'd,
Waved triumph o'er the proftrate world,
Infcribed with inconfiftent types
Of liberty and thirteen ftripes⁴.
Beneath, the croud without delay,
The dedication-rites effay,
And gladly pay in antient fafhion,
The ceremonies of libation;
While brifkly to each patriot lip
Walks eager round th' infpiring flip⁵:
Delicious draught, whofe pow'rs inherit
The quinteffence of public fpirit!
Which whofo taftes, perceives his mind
To nobler politics refined,
Or rouz'd for martial controverfy,
As from transforming cups of Circe⁶;
Or warm'd with Homer's nectar'd liquor,
That fill'd the veins of gods with ichor⁷.
At hand for new fupplies in ftore,
The tavern opes its friendly door,
Whence to and fro the waiters run,
Like bucket-men at fires in town⁸.

       Then

Then with three shouts that tore the sky,
'Tis consecrate to Liberty;
To guard it from th' attacks of Tories,
A grand committee cull'd of four is,
Who foremost on the patriot spot,
Had brought the flip and paid the shot.

By this, M'Fingal with his train,
Advanc'd upon th' adjacent plain,
And fierce with loyal rage possess'd,
Pour'd forth the zeal, that fired his breast.
"What madbrain'd rebel gave commission,
To raise this Maypole[9] of sedition!
Like Babel rear'd by bawling throngs,
With like confusion too of tongues[10],
To point at heav'n and summon down,
The thunders of the British crown[11]?
Say will this paltry pole secure
Your forfeit heads from Gage's pow'r?
Attack'd by heroes brave and crafty,
Is this to stand your ark of safety?
Or driv'n by Scottish laird and laddie[12],
Think ye to rest beneath its shadow?

When bombs, like fiery serpents, fly
And balls move hissing thro' the sky,
Will this vile pole, devote to freedom,
Save like the Jewish pole in Edom;
Or, like the brazen snake of Moses[13],
Cure your crack't skulls and batter'd noses?
Ye dupes to ev'ry factious rogue,
Or tavernprating demagogue,
Whose tongue but rings, with sound more full,
On th' empty drumhead of his skull,
Behold you know not what noisy fools
Use you, worse simpletons, for tools?
For Liberty in your own by-sense
Is but for crimes a patent licence;
To break of law th' Egyptian yoke,
And throw the world in common stock,
Reduce all grievances and ills
To Magna Charta[14] of your wills,
Establish cheats and frauds and nonsense,
Fram'd by the model of your conscience,
Cry justice down, as out of fashion
And fix its scale of depreciation[15],

Defy all creditors to trouble ye,
And pass new years of Jewish jubilee;
Drive judges out, like Aaron's calves,
By jurisdictions of white staves[17],
And make the bar and bench and steeple,
Submit t' our sov'reign Lord, the people;
Assure each knave his whole assets,
By gen'ral amnesty of debts;
By plunder rise to pow'r and glory,
And brand all property as tory[18];
Expose all wares to lawful seizures
Of mobbers and monopolizers;
Break heads and windows and the peace,
For your own int'rest and increase;
Dispute and pray and fight and groan,
For public good, and mean your own;
Prevent the laws, by fierce attacks,
From quitting scores upon your backs,
Lay your old dread, the gallows, low,
And seize the stocks[19] your antient foe;
And turn them, as convenient engines
To wreak your patriotic vengeance;

        While

While all, your claims who underſtand,
Confeſs they're in the owner's hand:
And when by clamours and confuſions,
Your freedom's grown a public nuiſance,
Cry, Liberty, with pow'rful yearning,
As he does, fire, whoſe houſe is burning,
Tho' he already has much more,
Than he can find occaſion for.
While every dunce, that turns the plains
Tho' bankrupt in eſtate and brains,
By this new light transform'd to traitor,
Forſakes his plow to turn dictator,
Starts an haranguing chief of Whigs,
And drags you by the ears, like pigs.
All bluſter arm'd with factious licence,
Transform'd at once to politicians;
Each leather-apron'd clown grown wiſe,
Preſents his forward face t' adviſe,
And tatter'd legiſlators meet
From ev'ry workſhop thro' the ſtreet;
His gooſe the tailor finds new uſe in,
To patch and turn the conſtitution;

The

The blackfmith comes with fledge and grate,
To ironbind the wheels of ftate;
The quack forbears his patient's foufe,
To purge the Council and the Houfe,
The tinker quits his molds and doxies,
To caft affembly-men at proxies[20].
From dunghills deep of fable hue,
Your dirtbred patriots fpring to view,
To wealth and pow'r and penfion rife,
Like new-wing'd maggots chang'd to flies;
And fluttring round in proud parade
Strut in the robe, or gay cockade.
See Arnold quits for ways more certain,
His bankrupt perj'ries for his fortune,
Brews rum no longer in his ftore,
Jockey and fkipper now no more;
Forfakes his warehoufes and docks,
And writs of flander for the pox,
And purg'd by patriotifm from fhame,
Grows Gen'ral of the foremoft name[21].

HIATUS[22].

For in this ferment of the stream,
The dregs have work'd up to the brim,
And by the rule of topsyturvys,
The skum stands swelling on the surface.
You've caus'd your pyramid t' ascend
And set it on the little end;
Like Hudibras [23], your empire's made,
Whose crupper had o'ertopped his head;
You've push'd and turn'd the whole world up-
Side down and got yourselves a-top:
While all the great ones of your state,
Are crush'd beneath the pop'lar weight,
Nor can you boast this present hour,
The shadow of the form of pow'r.
For what's your Congress, or its end?
A power t' advise and·recommend;
To call for troops, adjust your quotas,
And yet no soul is bound to notice [24];
To pawn your faith to th' utmost limit,
But cannot bind you to redeem it [25],
And when in want no more in them lies,
Than begging of your State-Assemblies;

Can

Can utter oracles of dread,
Like friar Bacon's brazen head [26],
But should a faction e'er dispute 'em,
Has ne'er an arm to execute 'em.
As tho' you chose supreme dictators,
And put them under confervators;
You've but pursued the selfsame way,
With Shakespeare's Trinclo in the play [27],
" You shall be viceroys here, 'tis true,
But we'll be viceroys over you."
What wild confusion hence must ensue,
Tho' common danger yet cements you;
So some wreck'd vessel, all in shatters,
Is held up by surrounding waters,
But stranded, when the pressure ceases,
Falls by its rottenness to pieces.
And fall it must—if wars were ended,
You'll ne'er have sense enough to mend it;
But creeping on with low intrigues
Like vermin of an hundred legs [23],
Will find as short a life assign'd,
As all things else of reptile kind.

Your

Your Commonwealth's a common harlot,
The property of ev'ry varlet,
Which now in taste and full employ,
All forts admire, as all enjoy;
But foon a batter'd strumpet grown,
You'll curse and drum her out of town.
Such is the government you chose,
For this you bade the world be foes,
For this so mark'd for dissolution,
You scorn the British constitution[29],
That constitution, form'd by sages,
The wonder of all modern ages:
Which owns no failure in reality,
Except corruption and venality;
And only proves the adage just,
That best things spoil'd corrupt to worst.
So man supreme in mortal station,
And mighty lord of this creation,
When once his corse is dead as herring,
Becomes the most offensive carrion,
And sooner breeds the plague, 'tis found,
Than all beasts rotting 'bove the ground.

Yet

Yet for this gov'rnment, to difmay us,
You've call'd up anarchy from chaos,
With all the followers of her fchool,
Uproar and rage and wild mifrule;
For whom this rout of Whigs diftracted
And ravings dire of ev'ry crack'd head;
Thefe new-caft legiflative engines
Of county-mufters and conventions,
Committees vile of correfpondence[30],
And mobs, whofe tricks have almoft undone 's;
While reafon fails to check your courfe,
And loyalty's kick'd out of doors,
And folly, like inviting landlord,
Hoifts on your poles her royal ftandard.
While the king's friends in doleful dumps,
Have worn their courage to the ftumps,
And leaving George in fad difafter,
Moft finfully deny their mafter.
What furies raged when you in fea,
In fhape of Indians drown'd the tea[31],
When your gay fparks, fatigued to watch it[32],
Affumed the moggifon[33] and hatchet.

With

With wampom'd blankets hid their laces[34],
And like their sweethearts, primed their faces[35]:
While not a redcoat[36] dar'd oppose,
And scarce a Tory show'd his nose,
While Hutchinson for sure retreat,
Manouvred to his country seat,
And thence affrighted in the suds,
Stole off bareheaded thro' the woods[37]!
Have you not rous'd your mobs to join,
And make Mandamus-men resign[38],
Call'd forth each duffil-dress'd curmudgeon,
With dirty trowsers and white bludgeon,
Forc'd all our Councils thro' the land,
To yield their necks to your command[39];
While paleness marks their late disgraces
Thro' all their rueful length of faces?
Have you not caused as woful work,
In loyal city of New York[40],
When all the rabble well cockaded,
In triumph thro' the streets paraded;
And mobb'd the Tories, scared their spouses,
And ransack'd all the custom-houses[41],

Made such a tumult, bluster, jarring,
That mid the clash of tempests warring,
Smith's weathercock[42] with veers forlorn,
Could hardly tell which way to turn;
Burnt effigies of th' higher powers[43],
Contriv'd in planetary hours,
As witches with clay-images,
Destroy or torture whom they please;
Till fired with rage, th' ungrateful club
Spared not your best friend, Belzebub[44],
O'erlook'd his favours and forgot
The rev'rence due his cloven foot,
And in the selfsame furnace frying,
Burn'd him and North and Bute and Tryon[45]
Did you not in as vile and shallow way,
Fright our poor Philadelphian, Galloway,
Your Congress when the daring ribald
Belied, berated and bescribbled?
What ropes and halters did you send,
Terrific emblems of his end,
Till least he'd hang in more than effigy,
Fled in a fog the trembling refugee[46]?

Now

Now rising in progression fatal,
Have you not ventur'd to give battle?
When treason chaced our heroes troubled,
With rusty gun and leathern doublet,
Turn'd all stonewalls and groves and bushes,
To batt'ries arm'd with blunderbusses,
And with deep wounds that fate portend,
Gaul'd many a reg'lar's latter end,
Drove them to Boston, as in jail,
Confined without mainprize or bail[47].
Were not these deeds enough betimes,
To heap the measure of your crimes,
But in this loyal town and dwelling,
You raise these ensigns of rebellion?
'Tis done; fair Mercy shuts her door;
And Vengeance now shall sleep no more[48];
Rise then, my friends, in terror rise,
And wipe this scandal from the skies!
You'll see their Dagon[49], tho' well jointed,
Will sink before the Lord's anointed[50],
And like old Jericho's proud wall,
Before our ram's horns prostrate fall[51]."

This

This said, our 'Squire, yet undismay'd
Call'd forth the Constable to aid,
And bade him read in nearer station,
The riot-act and proclamation;
Who now advancing tow'rd the ring,
Began, " Our sov'reign Lord the King "—[52]
When thousand clam'rous tongues he hears,
And clubs and stones assail his ears;
To fly was vain, to fight was idle,
By foes encompass'd in the middle;
In stratagem his aid he found,
And fell right craftily to ground;
Then crept to seek an hiding place,
'Twas all he could, beneath a brace;
Where soon the conq'ring crew espied him
And where he lurk'd, they caught and tied him.

At once with resolution fatal,
Both Whigs and Tories rush'd to battle;
Instead of weapons, either band
Seiz'd on such arms, as came to hand.
And as fam'd Ovid paints th' adventures
Of wrangling Lapithæ and Centaurs[53],

Who at their feaft, by Bacchus[54] led,
Threw bottles at each other's head,
And thefe arms failing in their fcuffles,
Attack'd with handirons, tongs and fhovels:
So clubs and billets, ftaves and ftones
Met fierce, encount'ring ev'ry fconce,
And cover'd o'er with knobs and pains
Each void receptacle for brains;
Their clamours rend the hills around,
And earth rebellows with the found;
And many a groan increas'd the din
From broken nofe and batter'd fhin.
M'Fingal rifing at the word,
Drew forth his old militia fword;
Thrice cried, "King George," as erft in diftrefs
Romancing heroes did their miftrefs,
And brandifhing the blade in air,
Struck terror thro' th' oppofing war.
The Whigs, unfafe within the wind
Of fuch commotion fhrunk behind.
With whirling fteel around addrefs'd,
Fierce thro' their thickeft throng he prefs'd,

(Who roll'd on either fide in arch,
Like Red-fea waves in Ifrael's march)
And like a meteor rufhing through,
Struck on their pole a vengeful blow.
Around, the Whigs, of clubs and ftones
Difcharg'd whole vollies in platoons,
That o'er in whiftling terror fly,
But not a foe dares venture nigh.
And now perhaps with conqueft crown'd,
Our 'Squire had fell'd their pole to ground;
Had not fome Pow'r, a Whig at heart,
Defcended down and took their part;
(Whether 'twere Pallas[55], Mars[56], or Iris[57],
'Tis fcarce worth while to make enquiries)
Who at the nick of time alarming,
Affumed the graver form of Chairman;
Addrefs'd a Whig, in ev'ry fcene
The ftouteft wreftler on the green,
And pointed where the fpade was found,
Late ufed to fix their pole in ground,
And urg'd with equal arms and might
To dare our 'Squire to fingle fight[58].

The

The Whig thus arm'd, untaught to yield,
Advanc'd tremendous to the field;
Nor did M'Fingal shun the foe,
But stood to brave the desp'rate blow;
While all the party gaz'd suspended,
To see the deadly combat ended.
And Jove in equal balance weigh'd
The sword against the brandish'd spade,
He weigh'd; but lighter than a dream,
The sword flew up and kick'd the beam,
Our 'Squire on tiptoe rising fair,
Lifts high a noble stroke in air,
Which hung not, but like dreadful engines
Descended on the foe in vengeance.
But ah, in danger with dishonor
The sword perfidious fails its owner;
That sword, which oft had stood its ground
By huge trainbands encompass'd round,
Or on the bench, with blade right loyal[59],
Had won the day at many a trial,
Of stones and clubs had brav'd th' alarms,
Shrunk from these new Vulcanian arms[60].

The

The spade so temper'd from the sledge,
Nor keen nor solid harm'd its edge,
Now met it from his arm of might
Descending with steep force to smite[61];
The blade snapp'd short—and from his hand
With rust embrown'd the glitt'ring sand.
Swift turn'd M'Fingal at the view,
And call'd for aid th' attendant crew,
In vain; the Tories all had run,
When scarce the fight was well begun;
Their setting wigs he saw decreas'd
Far in th' horizon tow'rd the west.
Amaz'd he view'd the shameful sight,
And saw no refuge but in flight:
But age unweildy check'd his pace,
Tho' fear had wing'd his flying race;
For not a trifling prize at stake;
No less than great M'Fingal's back.
With legs and arms he work'd his course,
Like rider that outgoes his horse,
And labour'd hard to get away, as
Old Satan struggling on thro' chaos[62]:

Till

Till looking back he fpied in rear
The fpade-arm'd chief advanc'd too near.
Then ftopp'd and feiz'd a ftone that lay,
An antient land-mark near the way;
Nor fhall we, as old Bards have done,
Affirm it weigh'd an hundred ton [63]:
But fuch a ftone as at a fhift
A modern might fuffice to lift,
Since men, to credit their enigmas,
Are dwindled down to dwarfs and pigmies,
And giants exiled with their cronies,
To Brobdingnags and Patagonias [64].
But while our hero turn'd him round,
And ftoop'd to raife it from the ground,
The deadly fpade difcharg'd a blow
Tremendous on his rear below:
His bent knee fail'd, and void of ftrength,
Stretch'd on the ground his manly length;
Like antient oak o'erturn'd he lay,
Or tow'rs to tempefts fall'n a prey,
And more things elfe—but all men know 'em,
If flightly vers'd in Epic Poem.

At once the crew, at this sad crisis,
Fail on and bind him ere he rises,
And with loud shouts and joyful soul
Conduct him pris'ner to the pole.

When now the Mob in lucky hour,
Had got their en'mies in their pow'r,
They first proceed by wise command
To take the constable in hand.
Then from the pole's sublimest top
They speeded to let down the rope,
At once its other end in haste bind,
And make it fast upon his waistband,
Till like the earth, as stretch'd on tenter,
He hung self-balanc'd on his center[65].
Then upwards all hands hoisting sail,
They swung him, like a keg of ale,
Till to the pinnacle so fair,
He rose like meteor in the air.
As Socrates of old at first did
To aid philosophy get hoisted,
And found his thoughts flow strangely clear,
Swung in a basket in mid air[66]:

Our

Our culprit thus in purer fky,
With like advantage rais'd his eye;
And looking forth in profpect wide
His Tory errors clearly fpied,
And from his elevated ftation,
With bawling voice began addreffing.
" Good gentlemen and friends and kin,
For heav'n's fake hear, if not for mine!
I here renounce the Pope, the Turks,
The King, the Devil and all their works;
And will, fet me but once at eafe,
Turn Whig or Chriftian, what you please;
And always mind your laws as juftly;
Should I live long as old Methus'lah,
I'll never join with Britifh rage,
Nor help Lord North, or Gen'ral Gage,
Nor lift my gun in future fights,
Nor take away your charter'd rights,
Nor overcome your new-rais'd levies,
Deftroy your towns, nor burn your navies,
Nor cut your poles down while I've breath,
Tho' rais'd more thick than hatchel-teeth [67]:

But

But leave king George and all his elves
To do their conq'ring work themselves."

This said, they lower'd him down in state,
Spread at all points, like falling cat;
But took a vote first on the question,
That they'd accept this full confession,
And to their fellowship and favor,
Restore him on his good behaviour.

Not so, our 'Squire submits to rule,
But stood heroic as a mule.
"You'll find it all in vain, quoth he,
To play your rebel tricks on me.
All punishments the world can render,
Serve only to provoke th' offender;
The will's confirm'd by treatment horrid,
As hides grow harder when they're curried.
No man e'er felt the halter draw,
With good opinion of the law;
Or held in method orthodox
His love of justice in the stocks[68];

Or fail'd to lofe by sheriff's shears
At once his loyalty and ears[69].
Have you made Murray[70] look less big,
Or smoak'd old Williams to a Whig[71]?
Did our mobb'd Oliver[72] quit his station,
Or heed his vows of resignation?
Has Rivington, in dread of stripes,
Ceas'd lying since you stole his types[73]?
And can you think my faith will alter,
By tarring, whipping, or the halter?
I'll stand the worst; for recompence
I trust King George and Providence.
And when, our conquest gain'd, I come,
Array'd in law and terror home,
You'll rue this inauspicious morn,
And curse the day you e'er were born,
In Job's high style of imprecations,
With all his plagues, without his patience."

 Meanwhile beside the pole, the guard
A Bench of Justice had prepar'd,
Where sitting round in awful sort,
The grand Committee hold their court[74];

        While

While all the crew in silent awe,
Wait from their lips the lore of law.
Few moments with deliberation,
They hold the solemn consultation,
When soon in judgment all agree,
And Clerk declares the dread decree;
" That 'Squire M'Fingal having grown,
The vilest Tory in the town,
And now on full examination,
Convicted by his own confession,
Finding no tokens of repentance,
This Court proceed to render sentence:
That first the Mob a slip-knot single
Tie round the neck of said M'Fingal;
And in due form do tar him next,
And feather, as the law directs;
Then thro' the town attendant ride him,
In cart with Constable beside him,
And having held him up to shame,
Bring to the pole from whence he came [15]."

 Forthwith the croud proceed to deck
With halter'd noose M'Fingal's neck,
       While

While he, in peril of his foul,
Stood tied half-hanging to the pole;
Then lifting high the pond'rous jar,
Pour'd o'er his head the fmoaking tar:
With lefs profufion erft was fpread
The Jewish oil on royal head [76],
That down his beard and veftments ran,
And cover'd all his outward man.
As when (fo Claudian fings) the Gods
And earth-born giants fell at odds [77],
The ftout Enceladus [78] in malice
Tore mountains up to throw at Pallas;
And as he held them o'er his head,
The river from their fountains fed,
Pour'd down his back its copious tide,
And wore its channels in his hyde:
So from the high rais'd urn the torrents,
Spread down his fide their various currents;
His flowing wig, as next the brim,
Firft met and drank the fable ftream;
Adown his vifage ftern and grave,
Roll'd and adhered the vifcid wave;

With arms depending as he ſtood,
Each cuff capacious holds the flood;
From noſe and chin's remoteſt end,
The tarry icicles depend;
Till all o'erſpread, with colors gay
He glitter'd to the weſtern ray,
Like fleet-bound trees in wintry ſkies,
Or Lapland idol carv'd in ice.
And now the feather-bag diſplay'd,
Is wav'd in triumph o'er his head,
And ſpreads him o'er with feathers miſſive,
And down upon the tar adheſive:
Not Maia's ſon, with wings for ears[79],
Such plumes around his viſage wears;
Nor Milton's ſix wing'd angel[80] gathers,
Such ſuperfluity of feathers.
Till all compleat appears our 'Squire
Like Gorgon or Chimera dire[81];
Nor more could boaſt on Plato's plan
To rank amid the race of man,
Or prove his claim to human nature,
As a two-legg'd, unfeather'd creature[82].

Then

Then on the two-wheel'd car of ſtate,
They rais'd our grand Duumvirate[83].
And as at Rome a like committee,
That found an owl within their city,
With ſolemn rites and ſad proceſſions,
At ev'ry ſhrine perform'd luſtrations;
And leaſt infection ſhould abound
From prodigy with face ſo round,
All Rome attends him thro' the ſtreet,
In triumph to his country-ſeat[84];
With like devotion all the choir
Paraded round our feather'd 'Squire;
In front the martial muſic comes
Of horns and fiddles, fifes and drums,
With jingling ſound of carriage bells,
And treble creak of ruſted wheels;
Behind, the croud in lengthen'd row,
With grave proceſſion cloſed the ſhow;
And at fit periods ev'ry throat
Combined in univerſal ſhout,
And hail'd great Liberty in chorus,
Or bawl'd, Confuſion to the Tories.

Not louder storm the welkin braves,
From clamors of conflicting waves;
Less dire in Lybian wilds the noise
When rav'ning lions lift their voice;
Or triumphs at town-meetings made,
On passing votes to reg'late trade[85].

Thus having borne them round the town,
Last at the pole they set them down,
And tow'rd the tavern take their way,
To end in mirth the festal day.

And now the Mob dispers'd and gone,
Left 'Squire and Constable alone.
The Constable in rueful case
Lean'd sad and solemn o'er a brace.
And fast beside him, cheek by jowl,
Stuck 'Squire M'Fingal 'gainst the pole,
Glued by the tar t' his rear applied,
Like barnacle[86] on vessel's side.
But tho' his body lack'd physician,
His spirit was in worse condition.

He

He found his fears of whips and ropes,
By many a drachm outweigh'd his hopes.
As men in goal without mainprize,
View ev'ry thing with other eyes,
And all goes wrong in church and ſtate,
Seen thro' perſpective of the grate:
So now M'Fingal's ſecond-ſight
Beheld all things in diff'rent light;
His viſual nerve, well purg'd with tar,
Saw all the coming ſcenes of war.
As his prophetic ſoul grew ſtronger,
He found he could hold in no longer;
Firſt from the pole, as fierce he ſhook,
His wig from pitchy durance broke,
His mouth unglued, his feathers flutter'd,
His tarr'd ſkirts crack'd, and thus he utter'd,
" Ah, Mr. Conſtable, in vain
We ſtrive 'gainſt wind and tide and rain!
Behold my doom! this feather'd omen
Portends what diſmal times are coming.
Now future ſcenes before my eyes,
And ſecond-ſighted forms ariſe;
       I hear

I hear a voice that calls away,
And cries, the Whigs will win the day[87];
My beck'ning Genius gives command,
And bids us fly the fatal land;
Where changing name and conſtitution,
Rebellion turns to revolution[88],
While Loyalty oppreſs'd in tears,
Stands trembling for its neck and ears.
Go, ſummon all our brethren greeting,
To muſter at our uſual meeting.
There my prophetic voice ſhall warn 'em,
Of all things future that concern 'em,
And ſcenes diſcloſe on which, my friend,
Their conduct and their lives depend:
There I—but firſt 'tis more of uſe,
From this vile pole to ſet me looſe;
Then go with cautious ſteps and ſteady,
While I ſteer home and make all ready."

END OF CANTO THIRD.

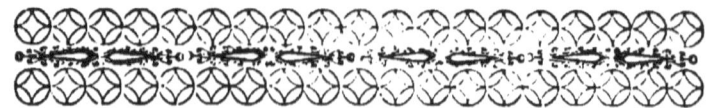

M'FINGAL:

CANTO FOURTH,

OR

THE VISION.

NOW night came down, and rose full soon
    That patroness of rogues, the Moon;
Beneath whose kind, protecting ray
Wolves, brute and human, prowl for prey.
The honest world all snored in chorus,
While owls, and ghosts and thieves and Tories,
Whom erst the mid-day sun had aw'd,
Crept from their lurking holes abroad.
On cautious hinges, slow and stiller
Wide oped the great M'Fingal's cellar [1],
Where shut from prying eyes in cluster,
The Tory Pandemonium [2] muster.

                              Their

Their chiefs all sitting round descried are,
On kegs of ale and seats of cyder;
When first M'Fingal dimly seen
Rose solemn from the turnep-bin³.
Nor yet his form had wholly lost
The original brightness it could boast⁴,
Nor less appear'd than Justice Quorum,
In feather'd majesty before 'em⁵.
Adown his tarstreak'd visage, clear
Fell glist'ning fast th' indignant tear,
And thus his voice, in mournful wise,
Pursued the prologue of his sighs.

" Brethren and friends, the glorious band
Of loyalty in rebel land!
It was not thus you've seen me sitting
Return'd in triumph from town-meeting,
When blustring Whigs were put to stand,
And votes obey'd my guiding hand,
And new commissions pleas'd my eyes;
Blest days, but ah, no more to rise!
Alas, against my better light
And optics sure of second-sight⁶,

My stubborn soul in error strong,
Had faith in Hutchinson[7] too long.
See what brave trophies still we bring
From all our battles for the king;
And yet these plagues now past before us,
Are but our entring wedge of sorrows.
I see in glooms tempestuous stand
The cloud impending o'er the land;
That cloud, which still beyond their hopes
Serves all our orators with tropes,
Which tho' from our own vapors fed,
Shall point its thunders on our head!
I see the Mob, beflipp'd[8] in taverns,
Hunt us, like wolves, thro' wilds and caverns!
What dungeons rise t' alarm our fears,
What horsewhips whistle round our ears!
Tar yet in embryo in the pine[9]
Shall run, on Tories backs to shine;
Trees rooted fair in groves of fallows
Are growing for our future gallows;
And geese unhatch'd, when pluck'd in fray,
Shall rue the feath'ring of that day[10].

For me, before these fatal days
I mean to fly th' accursed place,
And follow omens, which of late
Have warn'd me of impending fate;
Yet pass'd unnoticed o'er my view,
Till sad conviction proved them true;
As prophecies of best intent,
Are only heeded in th' event.

For late in visions of the night
The gallows stood before my sight;
I saw its ladder heav'd on end;
I saw the deadly rope descend;
And in its noose that wav'ring swang,
Friend Malcolm[11] hung, or seem'd to hang.
How changed from him, who bold as lyon,
Stood Aid-de-Camp to Governor Tryon,
Made rebels vanish once, like witches,
And saved his life, but dropp'd his breeches[12].
I scarce had made a fearful bow,
And trembling ask'd him, "How d'ye do."
When lifting up his eyes so wide,
His eyes alone, his hands were tied;

With

With feeble voice, as spirits use,
Now almost choak'd with gripe of noose;
" Ah [13] fly, my friend, he cried, escape,
And keep yourself from this sad scrape;
Enough you've talk'd and writ and plann'd;
The Whigs have got the upper hand.
Dame Fortune's wheel has turn'd so short,
It plung'd us fairly in the dirt;
Could mortal arm our fears have ended,
This arm (and shook it) had defended.
But longer now 'tis vain to stay;
See ev'n the Reg'lars run away:
Wait not till things grow desperater,
For hanging is no laughing matter:
This might your grandsires' fortunes tell you on
Who both were hang'd the last rebellion [14];
Adventure then no longer stay,
But call your friends and run away.
For lo, thro' deepest glooms of night
I come to aid thy second-fight,
Disclose the plagues that round us wait
And wake the dark decrees of fate.

Ascend

Afcend this ladder whence unfurl'd
The curtain opes of t'other world,
For here new worlds their fcenes unfold,
Seen from this backdoor of the old [15].
As when Æneas [16] rifqued his life,
Like Orpheus vent'ring for his wife [17],
And bore in fhow his mortal carcafe,
Thro' realms of Erebus and Orcus [18],
Then in the happy fields Elyfian,
Saw all his embryon fons in vifion:
As fhown by great archangel, Michael,
Old Adam faw the world's whole fequel,
And from the mount's extended fpace,
The rifing fortunes of his race [19];
So from this ftage fhalt thou behold,
The war its coming fcenes unfold,
Rais'd by my arm to meet thine eye;
My Adam, thou, thine Angel, I.
But firft my pow'r for vifions bright,
Muft cleanfe from clouds thy mental fight,
Remove the dim fuffufions fpread,
Which bribes and fal'ries there have bred;

And

And from the well of Bute infuse,
Three genuine drops of Highland dews,
To purge, like euphrasy and rue[20],
Thine eyes, for much thou hast to view.

Now freed from Tory darkness raise
Thy head and spy the coming days;
For lo before our second-sight,
The Continent ascends in light;
From north to south what gath'ring swarms,
Increase the pride of rebel arms!
Thro' ev'ry State our legions brave,
Speed gallant marches to the grave,
Of battling Whigs the frequent prize,
While rebel trophies stain the skies[21].
Behold o'er northern realms afar,
Extend the kindling flames of war!
See fam'd St. John's and Montreal,
Doom'd by Montgom'ry's arm to fall[22]!
Where Hudson with majestic sway,
Thro' hills disparted plows his way;
Fate spreads on Bemus' Heights alarms,
And pours destruction on our arms[23];

There

There Bennington's enfanguin'd plain[24].
And Stony-Point, the prize of Wayne[25].
Behold near Del'ware's icy roar,
Where morning dawns on Trenton's fhore,
While Heffians fpread their Chriftmas feafts,
Rufh rude thefe uninvited guefts;
Nor aught avail, to Whigs a prize,
Their martial whifkers' grifly fize[26].
On Princeton plains our heroes yield,
And fpread in flight the vanquifh'd field,
While fear to Mawhood's heels puts on
Wings, wide as worn by Maia's fon[27].
Behold the Pennfylvanian fhore,
Enrich'd with ftreams of Britifh gore[28];
Where many a vet'ran chief in bed
Of honor refts his flumbring head,
And in foft vales in land of foes,
Their wearied virtue finds repofe[29].
See plund'ring Dunmore's negro band
Fly headlong from Virginia's ftrand[30];
And far on fouthern hills our coufins,
The Scotch M'Donalds fall by dozens[31];

Or where King's Mountain lifts its head,
Our ruin'd bands in triumph led[32]!
Behold o'er Tarlton's bluft'ring train,
The Rebels ftretch the captive chain[33]!
Afar near Eutaw's fatal fprings
Defcending Vict'ry fpreads her wings[34]!
Thro' all the land in various chace,
We hunt the rainbow of fuccefs;
In vain! their Chief fuperior ftill
Eludes our force with Fabian fkill[35],
Or fwift defcending by furprize,
Like Pruffia's eagle fweeps the prize."

I look'd, nor yet, oppreft with fears,
Gave credit to my eyes or ears,
But held the views an empty dream,
On Berkley's immaterial fcheme[36];
And pondring fad with troubled breaft
At length my rifing doubts exprefs'd.
" Ah whither, thus by rebels fmitten,
Is fled th' omnipotence of Britain[37],
Or fail'd its ufual guard to keep,
Gone truanting or fall'n afleep;

As Baal his prophets left confounded,
And bawling vot'ries gafh'd and wounded [38]?
Did not, retir'd to bow'rs Elyfian,
Great Mars leave with her his commiffion,
And Neptune erft in treaty free,
Give up dominion o'er the fea [39]?
Elfe where's the faith of famed orations [40],
Addrefs, debate and proclamations,
Or courtly fermon, laureat ode,
And ballads on the watry God [41];
With whofe high ftrains great George enriches
His eloquence of gracious fpeeches [42]?
Not faithful to our Highland eyes,
Thefe deadly forms of vifion rife;
But fure fome Whig-infpiring fprite
Now palms delufion on our fight.
I'd fcarcely truft a tale fo vain,
Should revelation prompt the ftrain,
Or Offian's ghoft the fcenes rehearfe,
In all the melody of Erfe." [43]

" Too long, quoth Malcolm, with confufion
You've dwelt already in delufion,

As

As Sceptics, of all fools the chief,
Hold faith in creeds of unbelief.
I come to draw thy veil aside
Of error, prejudice and pride.
Fools love deception, but the wife
Prefer sad truths to pleasing lies.
For know those hopes can ne'er succeed
That trust on Britain's breaking reed.
For weak'ning long from bad to worse
By fatal atrophy of purse,
She feels at length with trembling heart,
Her foes have found her mortal part.
As famed Achilles, dipped by Thetis
In Styx, as sung in antient ditties,
Grew all caseharden'd o'er like steel,
Invulnerable, save his heel[44],
And laugh'd at swords and spears, as squibs,
And all diseases, but the kibes[5];
Yet met at last his fatal wound,
By Paris' arrow nail'd to ground[46]:
So Britain's boasted strength deserts,
In these her empire's utmost skirts,

Remov'd

Remov'd beyond her fierce impreffions,
And atmofphere of omniprefence;
Nor to thefe fhores remoter ends,
Her dwarf omnipotence extends:
Whence in this turn of things fo ftrange,
'Tis time our principles to change.
For vain that boafted faith, which gathers
No perquifite, but tar and feathers,
No pay, but Whig's infulting malice,
And no promotion, but the gallows.
I've long enough ftood firm and fteady,
Half hang'd for loyalty already:
And could I fave my neck and pelf
I'd turn a flaming Whig myfelf,
And quit this caufe and courfe and calling,
Like rats that fly from houfe that's falling.
But fince, obnoxious here to fate,
This faving wifdom comes too late,
Our nobleft hopes already croft,
Our fal'ries gone, our titles loft,
Doom'd to worfe fuff'rings from the mob
Than Satan's furg'ries ufed on Job [47];

What

What more remains but now with fleight,
What's left of us to fave by flight?

Now raife thine eyes for vifions true
Again afcending wait thy view."
I look'd and clad in early light,
The fpires of Bofton rofe to fight;
The morn o'er eaftern hills afar,
Illum'd the varying fcenes of war.
Great Howe had long fince in the lap
Of Loring taken out his nap,
And with the fun's afcending ray,
The cuckold came to take his pay[48].
When all th' encircling hills around,
With inftantaneous breaftworks crown'd,
With pointed thunders met his fight,
By magic rear'd the former night.
Each fummit, far as eye commands,
Shone peopled with rebellious bands[49].
Aloft their tow'ring heroes rife,
As Titans erft affail'd the fkies[50],
Leagued with fuperior force to prove,
The fcepter'd hand of Britifh Jove.

Mounds

Mounds piled on hills afcended fair
With batt'ries placed in middle air,
That rais'd like angry clouds on high
Seem'd like th' artill'ry of the fky,
And hurl'd their fiery bolts amain,
In thunder on the trembling plain.
I faw along the proftrate ftrand,
Our baffled Gen'rals quit the land,
And fwift as frighted mermaids flee,
T' our boafted element, the fea [51]!
Refign that long contefted fhore,
Again the prize of rebel-power,
And tow'rd their town of refuge fly,
Like convict Jews condemn'd to die [52].

Then tow'rd the north, I turn'd my eyes,
Where Saratoga's heights arife,
And faw our chofen vet'ran band,
Defcend in terror o'er the land [53];
T' oppofe this fury of alarms,
Saw all New-England wake to arms,
And ev'ry Yanky full of mettle,
Swarm forth, like bees at found of kettle [54].

Not Rome, when Tarquin raped Lucretia[55],
Saw wilder muft'ring of militia.
Thro' all the woods and plains of fight,
What mortal battles fill'd my fight,
While Britifh corfes ftrew'd the fhore,
And Hudfon ting'd his ftreams with gore!
What tongue can tell the difmal day,
Or paint the party-color'd fray;
When yeomen left their fields afar,
To plow the crimfon plains of war;
When zeal to fwords transformed their fhares,
And turn'd their pruning-hooks to fpears,
Chang'd tailor's geefe to guns and ball,
And ftretch'd to pikes the cobler's awl[56];
While hunters fierce like mighty Nimrod,
Made on our troops a daring inroad;
And levelling fquint on barrel round,
Brought our beau-officers to ground[57];
While rifle-frocks fent Gen'rals cap'ring,
And redcoats fhrunk from leathern apron,
And epaulette and gorget run
From whinyard brown and rufty gun:

                                      While

While funburnt wigs in high command,
Rufh furious on our frighted band,
And antient beards and hoary hair,
Like meteors ftream in troubled air [58].
With locks unfhorn not Samfon more
Made ufelefs all the fhow of war,
Nor fought with affes' jaw for rarity,
With more fuccefs or fingularity [59].
I faw our vet'ran thoufands yield
And pile their mufkets on the field,
And peafant guards in rueful plight
March off our captured bands from fight;
While ev'ry rebel-fife in play,
To Yanky-doodle tun'd its lay,
And like the mufic of the fpheres,
Mellifluous footh'd their vanquifh'd ears [60].

" Alas, faid I, what baleful ftar,
Sheds fatal influence on the war,
And who that chofen Chief of fame,
That heads this grand parade of fhame?"

" There fee how fate, great Malcolm cried,
Strikes with its bolts the tow'rs of pride.

Behold that martial Macaroni[61],
Compound of Phœbus and Bellona[62],
With warlike sword and singsong lay,
Equipp'd alike for feast or fray,
Where equal wit and valour join;
This, this is he, the famed Burgoyne[63]:
Who pawn'd his honor and commission,
To coax the Patriots to submission,
By songs and balls secure obedience,
And dance the ladies to allegiance[64].
Oft his camp muses he'll parade,
At Boston in the grand blockade,
And well invoked with punch of arrack,
Hold converse sweet in tent or barrack,
Inspired in more heroic fashion,
Both by his theme and situation;
While farce and proclamation grand,
Rise fair beneath his plastic hand[65].
For genius swells more strong and clear
When close confin'd, like bottled beer:
So Prior's wit gain'd greater pow'r,
By inspiration of the tow'r[66];

And

And Raleigh faſt in priſon hurl'd
Wrote all the hiſt'ry of the world[67]:
So Wilkes grew, while in goal he lay,
More patriotic ev'ry day,
But found his zeal, when not confin'd,
Soon ſink below the freezing point,
And public ſpirit once ſo fair,
Evaporate in open air[68].
But thou, great favorite of Venus,
By no ſuch luck ſhalt cramp thy genius;
Thy friendly ſtars till wars ſhall ceaſe,
Shall ward th' illfortune of releaſe,
And hold thee faſt in bonds not feeble,
In good condition ſtill to ſcribble.
Such merit fate ſhall ſhield from firing,
Bomb, carcaſe, langridge and cold iron,
Nor truſts thy doubly laurell'd head,
To rude aſſaults of flying lead.
Hence in this Saratogue retreat,
For pure good fortune thou'lt be beat;
Nor taken oft, releas'd or reſcued,
Paſs for ſmall change, like ſimple Preſcott[69];

But

But captured there, as fates befall,
Shalt stand thy hand for't, once for all.
Then raise thy daring thoughts sublime,
And dip thy conq'ring pen in rhyme,
And changing war for puns and jokes,
Write new Blockades and Maids of Oaks." [70]

This said, he turn'd, and saw the tale,
Had dyed my trembling cheeks with pale;
Then pitying in a milder vein
Pursued the visionary strain.

" Too much perhaps hath pain'd your views
Of vict'ries gain'd by rebel crews;
Now see the deeds not small or scanty,
Of British Valor and Humanity;
And learn from this auspicious fight,
How England's sons and friends can fight;
In what dread scenes their courage grows,
And how they conquer all their foes."

I look'd and saw in wintry skies
Our spacious prison-walls arise,

Where Britons all their captives taming,
Plied them with scourging, cold and famine;
Reduced to life's concluding stages,
By noxious food and plagues contagious.
Aloft the mighty Loring stood,
And thrived, like Vampyre, on their blood,
And counting all his gains arising,
Dealt daily rations out of poison.
Amid the dead that croud the scene,
The moving skeletons were seen [71].
At hand our troops in vaunting strains,
Insulted all their wants and pains,
And turn'd on all the dying tribe,
The bitter taunt and scornful gibe:
And British officers of might,
Triumphant at the joyful fight,
O'er foes disarm'd with courage daring,
Exhausted all their tropes of swearing.
Around all stain'd with rebel blood,
Like Milton's lazar house it stood [72],
Where grim Despair attended nurse,
And Death was Gov'rnor of the house.

         Amaz'd

Amaz'd I cried, "Is this the way,
That Britifh Valour wins the day?"
More had I faid, in ftrains unwelcome,
Till interrupted thus by Malcolm:
"Blame not, quoth he, but learn the reafon
Of this new mode of conq'ring treafon.
'Tis but a wife, politic plan,
To root out all the rebel-clan;
(For furely treafon ne'er can thrive,
Where not a foul is left alive:)
A fcheme, all other chiefs to furpafs,
And to do th' effectual work to purpofe.
For war itfelf is nothing further,
But th' art and myftery of murther[73],
And who moft methods has effay'd,
Is the beft Gen'ral of the trade,
And ftands Death's Plenipotentiary,
To conquer, poifon, ftarve and bury.
This Howe well knew, and thus began,
(Defpifing Carlton's coaxing plan,
Who kept his pris'ners well and merry,
And dealt them food like Commiffary,

And

And by paroles and ranfoms vain,
Difmifs'd them all to fight again :)[74]
Whence his firft captives with great fpirit,
He tied up for his troops to fire at[75],
And hoped they'd learn on foes thus taken,
To aim at rebels without fhaking.
Then wife in ftratagem he plann'd
The fure deftruction of the land,
Turn'd famine, ficknefs and defpair,
To ufeful enginry of war,
Inftead of cannon, mufket, mortar,
Ufed peftilence and death and torture,
Sent forth the fmall pox and the greate *,
To thin the land of ev'ry traitor,
And order'd out with like endeavour,
Detachments of the prifon-fever[77];
Spread defolation o'er their head,
And plagues in Providence's ftead,
Perform'd with equal fkill and beauty,
Th' avenging angel's tour of duty,
Brought all the elements to join,
And ftars t' affift the great defign,

As once in league with Kishon's brook,
Famed Israel's foes they fought and took[18].
Then proud to raise a glorious name,
And em'lous of his country's fame,
He bade these prison-walls arise,
Like temple tow'ring to the skies,
Where British Clemency renown'd,
Might fix her seat on sacred ground;
(That Virtue, as each herald saith,
Of whole blood kin to Punic Faith)[19]
Where all her Godlike pow'rs unveiling,
She finds a grateful shrine to dwell in.
Then at this altar for her honor,
Chose this Highpriest to wait upon her,
Who with just rites, in antient guises,
Presents these human sacrifices;
Great Loring, famed above laymen,
A proper Priest for Lybian Ammon,
Who, while Howe's gift his brows adorns,
Had match'd that deity in horns[60].
Here ev'ry day her vot'ries tell
She more devours than th' idol Bel[81];

       And

And thirsts more rav'nously for gore,
Than any worshipp'd Pow'r before.
That antient Heathen Godhead, Moloch,
Oft stay'd his stomach with a bullock,
Or if his morning rage you'd check first,
One child sufficed him for a breakfast[82];
But British Clemency with zeal
Devours her hundreds at a meal,
Right well by Nat'ralists defined,
A Being of carniv'rous kind.
So erst Gargantua pleas'd his palate,
And eat his pilgrims up for sallad[83].
Not blest with maw less ceremonious,
The wide-mouth'd whale that swallow'd Jonas[84];
Like earthquake gapes, to death devote,
That open sepulchre, her throat;
The grave, or barren womb you'd stuff,
And sooner bring to cry, enough;
Or fatten up to fair condition,
The leanflesh'd kine of Pharaoh's vision[85].

   Behold her temple where it stands
Erect by famed Britannic hands;

'Tis the blackhole of Indian ſtructure,
New-built with Engliſh architecture,
On plan, 'tis ſaid, contrived and wrote,
By Clive, before he cut his throat [86];
Who ere he took himſelf in hand,
Was her Highprieſt in Nabob-land [87]:
And when with conq'ring glory crown'd,
He'd well enſlav'd the nation round,
With pitying heart the gen'rous chief,
(Since ſlav'ry's worſe than loſs of life)
Bade deſolation circle far,
And famine end the work of war;
Thus looſed their chains and for their merits,
Diſmiſs'd them free to worlds of ſpirits:
Whence they with gratitude and praiſe,
Return'd to attend his latter days,
And hov'ring round his reſtleſs bed,
Spread nightly viſions o'er his head [88].

"Now turn, he cried, to nobler fights,
And mark the prowefs of our fights:
Behold like whelps of Britiſh Lyon,
The warriors, Clinton, Vaughan and Tryon [89],

March

March forth with patriotic joy,
To ravish, plunder, burn, destroy.
Great Gen'rals foremost in the nation,
The journeymen of Defolation!
Like Samson's foxes each assails,
Let loose with firebrands in their tails,
And spreads destruction more forlorn,
Than they did in Philistine corn[90].
And see in flames their triumphs rise,
Illuming all the nether skies,
And streaming, like a new Aurora,
The western hemisphere with glory!
What towns in ashes laid confess
These heroes' prowess and success!
What blacken'd walls, or burning fane,
For trophies spread the ruin'd plain!
What females caught in evil hour,
By force submit to British power,
Or plunder'd Negroes in disaster
Confess king George their lord and master!
What crimson corses strew their way
Till smoaking carnage dims the day!

Along

Along the shore for sure-reduction
They wield their besom of destruction.
Great Homer likens, in his Ilias,
To dogstar bright the fierce Achilles;
But ne'er beheld in red procession,
Three dogstars rise in constellation;
Or saw in glooms of ev'ning misty,
Such signs of fiery triplicity,
Which far beyond the comet's tail,
Portend destruction where they sail[91].
Oh had Great-Britain's godlike shore,
Produced but ten such heroes more,
They'd spared the pains and held the station,
Of this world's final conflagration,
Which when its time comes, at a stand,
Would find its work all done t' its hand!

Yet tho' gay hopes our eyes may bless;
Indignant fate forbids success;
Like morning dreams our conquest flies,
Disperf'd before the dawn arise."

Here

Here Malcolm paus'd; when pond'ring long,
Grief thus gave utt'rance to my tongue.
"Where shrink in fear our friends dismay'd,
And all the Tories' promis'd aid,
Can none amid these fierce alarms,
Assist the pow'r of royal arms?"
"In vain, he cried, our king depends,
On promis'd aid of Tory-friends[92].
When our own efforts want success,
Friends ever fail as fears increase.
As leaves in blooming verdure wove,
In warmth of summer cloath the grove,
But when autumnal frosts arise,
Leave bare their trunks to wintry skies;
So while your pow'r can aid their ends,
You ne'er can need ten thousand friends,
But once in want by foes dismay'd,
May advertise them stol'n or stray'd.
Thus ere Great-Britain's strength grew slack,
She gain'd that aid, she did not lack,
But now in dread, imploring pity,
All hear unmov'd her dol'rous ditty;

Allegiance

Allegiance wand'ring turns aftray,
And Faith grows dim for lack of pay
In vain fhe tries by new inventions,
Fear, falfhood, flatt'ry, threats and penfions,
Or fends Commifs'ners with credentials
Of promifes and penitentials[93].
As for his fare o'er Styx of old,
The Trojan ftole the bough of gold,
And leaft grim Cerberus fhould make head,
Stuff'd both his fobs with gingerbread[94];
Behold at Britain's utmoft fhifts,
Comes Johnftone loaded with like gifts,
To venture thro' the Whiggifh tribe,
To cuddle, wheedle, coax and bribe[95],
Enter their lands and on his journey,
Poffeffion take, as King's Attorney,
Buy all the vaffals to protect him,
And bribe the tenants not t' eject him :
And call to aid his defp'rate miffion,
His petticoated politician,
While Venus join'd t' affift the farce,
Strolls forth Embaffadrefs for Mars[96].

In vain he strives, for while he lingers,
These mastiffs bite his off'ring fingers;
Nor buys for George and realms infernal,
One spaniel, but the mongrel Arnold[97].

" 'Twere vain to paint in vision'd show,
The mighty nothings done by Howe;
What towns he takes in mortal fray,
As stations, whence to run away;
What conquests gain'd in battles warm,
To us no aid, to them no harm;
For still the event alike is fatal,
What'er success attend the battle,
If he gain victory, or lose it,
Who ne'er had skill enough to use it[99];
And better 'twere at their expence,
T' have drubb'd him into common sense,
And wak'd by bastings on his rear,
Th' activity, tho' but of fear.
By slow advance his arms prevail,
Like emblematic march of snail;
That be Millennium nigh or far,
'Twould long before him end the war.

From

From York to Philadelphian ground,
He sweeps the mighty flourish round,
Wheel'd circ'lar by excentric stars,
Like racing boys at prison-bars,
Who take the adverse crew in whole,
By running round the opp'site goal;
Works wide the traverse of his course,
Like ship in storms' opposing force,
Like millhorse circling in his race,
Advances not a single pace,
And leaves no trophies of reduction,
Save that of cankerworms, destruction.
Thus having long both countries curst,
He quits them, as he found them first,
Steers home disgraced, of little worth,
To join Burgoyne and rail at North [99].

Now raise thine eyes, and view with pleasure,
The triumphs of his famed successor."[100]
I look'd, and now by magic lore,
Faint rose to view the Jersey shore;
But dimly seen, in glooms array'd,
For Night had pour'd her sable shade,

And

And ev'ry ftar, with glimm'rings pale,
Was muffled deep in ev'ning veil :
Scarce vifible in dufky night,
Advancing redcoats rofe to fight ;
The lengthen'd train in gleaming rows
Stole filent from their flumb'ring foes,
Slow moved the baggage and the train,
Like fnail crept noifelefs o'er the plain ;
No trembling foldier dared to fpeak,
And not a wheel prefum'd to creak [101].
My looks my new furprize confefs'd
Till by great Malcolm thus addrefs'd : "
" Spend not thy wits in vain refearches ;
'Tis one of Clinton's moonlight marches.
From Philadelphia now retreating,
To fave his anxious troops a beating,
With hafty ftride he flies in vain,
His rear attack'd on Monmouth plain :
With various chance the mortal fray
Is lengthen'd to the clofe of day,
When his tired bands o'ermatch'd in fight,
Are refcued by defcending night [102] ;

He forms his camp with vain parade,
Till ev'ning spreads the world with shade,
Then still, like some endanger'd spark,
Steals off on tiptoe in the dark;
Yet writes his king in boasting tone,
How grand he march'd by light of moon [103].
I see him; but thou canst not; proud
He leads in front the trembling croud,
And wisely knows, if danger's near,
'Twill fall the heaviest on his rear [104].
Go on, great Gen'ral, nor regard
The scoffs of ev'ry scribling Bard,
Who sing how Gods that fatal night
Aided by miracles your flight,
As once they used, in Homer's day,
To help weak heroes run away;
Tell how the hours at awful trial,
Went back, as erst on Ahaz' dial,
While British Joshua stay'd the moon,
On Monmouth plains for Ajalon:
Heed not their sneers and gibes so arch,
Because she set before your march [105].

A small

A small mistake, your meaning right,
You take her influence for her light;
Her influence, which shall be your guide,
And o'er your Gen'ralship preside.
Hence still shall teem your empty skull,
With vict'ries when the moon's at full,
Which by transition yet more strange,
Wane to defeats before the change;
Hence all your movements, all your notions
Shall steer by like excentric motions,
Eclips'd in many a fatal crisis,
And dimm'd when Washington arises.
And see how Fate, herself turn'd traitor,
Inverts the antient course of nature,
And changes manners, tempers, climes,
To suit the genius of the times.
See Bourbon forms his gen'rous plan,
First guardian of the rights of man,
And prompt in firm alliance joins,
To aid the Rebels proud designs [100].
Behold from realms of eastern day,
His sails innum'rous shape their way.

In

In warlike line the billows sweep,
And roll the thunders of the deep [107].
See low in equinoctial skies,
The Western Islands fall their prize [108],
See British flags o'ermatch'd in might,
Put all their faith in instant flight,
Or broken squadrons from th' affray,
Drag flow their wounded hulks away.
Behold his chiefs in daring setts,
D'Estaings [109], De Grasses [110] and Fayettes [111],
Spread thro' our camps their dread alarms,
And swell the fears of rebel-arms.
Yet ere our empire sink in night,
One gleam of hope shall strike the sight;
As lamps that fail of oil and fire,
Collect one glimmering to expire.
And lo where southern shores extend,
Behold our union'd hosts descend,
Where Charlestown views with varying beams,
Her turrets gild th' encircling streams.
There by superior might compell'd,
Behold their gallant Lincoln yield,

Nor

Nor aught the wreaths avail him now,
Pluck'd from Burgoyne's imperious brow [112].
See furious from the vanquish'd strand,
Cornwallis leads his mighty band!
The southern realms and Georgian shore
Submit and own the victor's pow'r,
Lo, sunk before his wasting way,
The Carolinas fall his prey [113]!
In vain embattled hosts of foes
Essay in warring strife t' oppose.
See shrinking from his conq'ring eye,
The rebel legions fall or fly [114];
And with'ring in these torrid skies,
The northern laurel fades and dies [115].
With rapid force he leads his band
To fair Virginia's fated strand,
Triumphant eyes the travell'd zone,
And boasts the southern realms his own [116],
Nor yet this hero's glories bright
Blaze only in the fields of fight;
Not Howe's humanity more deserving,
In gifts of hanging and of starving;

Not Arnold plunders more tobacco,
Or steals more Negroes for Jamaica [117];
Scarce Rodney's self among th' Eustatians,
Insults so well the laws of nations [118];
Ev'n Tryon's fame grows dim, and mourning,
He yields the laurel crown of burning [119].
I see with rapture and surprize,
New triumphs sparkling in thine eyes.
But view where now renew'd in might,
Again the rebels dare the fight."

I look'd and far in southern skies,
Saw Greene, their second hope, arise,
And with his small but gallant band,
Invade the Carolinian land [120].
As winds in stormy circles whirl'd
Rush billowing o'er the darken'd world
And where their wasting fury roves,
Successive sweep th' astonish'd groves;
Thus where he pours the rapid fight,
Our boasted conquests sink in night,
And wide o'er all th' extended field,
Our forts resign, our armies yield,

Till

Till now regain'd the vanquish'd land,
He lifts his standard on the strand [121]:

Again to fair Virginia's coast,
I turn'd and view'd the British host.
Where Chesapeak's wide waters lave
Her shores and join th' Atlantic wave,
There fam'd Cornwallis tow'ring rose,
And scorn'd secure his distant foes;
His bands the haughty rampart raise,
And bid th' imperial standard blaze [122].
When lo, where ocean's bounds extend,
I saw the Gallic sails ascend,
With fav'ring breezes stem their way,
And croud with ships the spacious bay [123].
Lo Washington from northern shores,
O'er many a region, wheels his force,
And Rochambeau with legions bright,
Descends in terrors to the fight [124].
Not swifter cleaves his rapid way,
The eagle cow'ring o'er his prey,
Or knights in fam'd romance that fly
On fairy pinions thro' the sky.

Amaz'd

Amaz'd the Briton's startled pride,
Sees ruin wake on ev'ry side;
And all his troops to fate consign'd,
By instantaneous stroke Burgoyn'd [125].
Not Cadmus view'd with more surprize,
From earth embattled armies rise,
When by superior pow'r impell'd,
He sow'd with dragon's teeth the field [126].
Here Gallic troops in terror stand,
There rush in arms the Rebel band;
Nor hope remains from mortal fight,
Or that last British refuge, flight [127].
I saw with looks downcast and grave,
The Chief emerging from his cave [128],
(Where chaced like hare in mighty round,
His hunters earth'd him first in ground)
And doom'd by fate to rebel sway,
Yield all his captur'd hosts a prey [129].

There while I view'd the vanquish'd town,
Thus with a sigh my friend went on:
" Beholdst thou not that band forlorn,
Like slaves in Roman triumphs borne [130];

Their

Their faces length'ning with their fears,
And cheeks diftain'd with ftreams of tears,
Like dramatis perfonæ fage,
Equipt to act on Tyburn's ftage.
Lo thefe are they, who lur'd by follies,
Left all and follow'd great Cornwallis;
True to their King, with firm devotion,
For confcience fake and hop'd promotion,
Expectant of the promis'd glories,
And new Millennial ftate of Tories.
Alas, in vain, all doubts forgetting,
They tried th' omnipotence of Britain;
But found her arm, once ftrong and brave,
So fhorten'd now fhe cannot fave.
Not more aghaft departed fouls,
Who rifk'd their fate on Popifh bulls [131],
And find St. Peter at the wicket
Refufe to counterfign their ticket,
When driv'n to purgatory back,
With all their pardons in their pack:
Than Tories muft'ring at their ftations
On faith of royal proclamations [132].

As Pagan Chiefs at ev'ry crisis,
Confirm'd their leagues by facrifices,
And herds of beafts to all their deities,
Oblations fell at clofe of treaties:
Cornwallis thus in antient fafhion,
Concludes his league of cap'tulation,
And victims due to Rebel-glories,
Gives this an off'ring up of Tories.
See where reliev'd from fad embargo,
Steer off confign'd a recreant cargo,
Like old fcapegoats to roam in pain,
Mark'd like their great forerunner, Cain [133].
The reft, now doom'd by Britifh leagues,
To juftice of refentful Whigs,
Hold worthlefs lives on tenure ill,
Of tenancy at Rebel-will,
While hov'ring o'er their forfeit perfons,
The gallows waits his fure reverfions.

Thou too, M'Fingal, ere that day,
Shalt tafte the terrors of th' affray.
See o'er thee hangs in angry fkies,
Where Whiggifh conftellations rife,

And

And while plebeian figns afcend,
Their mob-infpiring afpects bend;
That baleful Star, whofe horrid hair [134]
Shakes forth the plagues of down and tar!
I fee the pole, that rears on high
Its flag terrific thro' the fky;
The Mob beneath prepar'd t' attack,
And tar predeftin'd for thy back!
Ah quit, my friend, this dang'rous home,
Nor wait the darker fcenes to come;
For know that Fate's aufpicious door,
Once fhut to flight is oped no more,
Nor wears its hinge by various ftations,
Like Mercy's door in proclamations [135].

But left thou paufe, or doubt to fly,
To ftranger vifions turn thine eye:
Each cloud that dimm'd thy mental ray,
And all the mortal mifts decay;
See more than human Pow'rs befriend,
And lo their hoftile forms afcend!
See tow'ring o'er th' extended ftrand,
The Genius of the weftern land,

In vengeance arm'd, his sword assumes,
And stands, like Tories, drest in plumes [136].
See o'er yon Council seat with pride,
How Freedom spreads her banners wide [137]!
There Patriotism with torch address'd,
To fire with zeal each daring breast!
While all the Virtues in their band,
Escape from yon unfriendly land,
Desert their antient British station,
Possest with rage of emigration.
Honor, his business at a stand,
For fear of starving quits their land;
And Justice, long disgraced at Court, had
By Mansfield's sentence been transported [138].
Vict'ry and Fame attend their way,
Tho' Britain wish their longer stay,
Care not what George or North [139] would be at,
Nor heed their writs of ne exeat [140];
But fired with love of colonizing,
Quit the fall'n empire for the rising."

   I look'd and saw with horror smitten,
These hostile pow'rs averse to Britain.

When lo, an awful fpectre rofe[141],
With languid palenefs on his brows;
Wan dropfies fwell'd his form beneath,
And iced his bloated cheeks with death;
His tatter'd robes expofed him bare,
To ev'ry blaft of ruder air;
On two weak crutches propt he ftood,
That bent at ev'ry ftep he trod,
Gilt titles graced their fides fo flender,
One, " Regulation," t'other, " Tender[142];"
His breaftplate grav'd with various dates,
" The faith of all th' United States[143]:"
Before him went his fun'ral pall,
His grave ftood dug to wait his fall.
I ftarted, and aghaft I cried,
" What means this fpectre at their fide?
What danger from a Pow'r fo vain,
And why he joins that fplendid train?"
" Alas, great Malcolm cried, experience
Might teach you not to truft appearance.
Here ftands, as dreft by fierce Bellona[144],
The ghoft of Continental Money[145],

Of dame Neceffity defcended,
With whom Credulity engender'd.
Tho' born with conftitution frail,
And feeble ftrength that foon muft fail;
Yet ftrangely vers'd in magic lore,
And gifted with transforming pow'r.
His fkill the wealth Peruvian joins
With diamonds of Brazilian mines [146].
As erft Jove fell by fubtle wiles
On Danae's apron thro' the tiles,
In fhow'rs of gold; [147] his potent hand
Shall fhed like fhow'rs thro' all the land.
Lefs great the magic art was reckon'd,
Of tallies caft by Charles the fecond,
Or Law's famed Miffiffipi fchemes [148],
Or all the wealth of Southfea dreams [149].
For he of all the world alone
Owns the longfought Philof'pher's ftone [150],
Reftores the fab'lous times to view,
And proves the tale of Midas true [151].
O'er heaps of rags, he waves his wand,
All turn to gold at his command,

Provide for prefent wants and future,
Raife armies, victual, clothe, accoutre,
Adjourn our conquefts by effoign,
Check Howe's advance and take Burgoyne,
Then makes all days of payment vain,
And turns all back to rags again [152].
In vain great Howe fhall play his part,
To ape and counterfeit his art:
In vain fhall Clinton, more belated,
A conj'rer turn to imitate it [153];
With like ill luck and pow'r as narrow,
They'll fare, like for'cers of old Pharaoh,
Who tho' the art they underftood
Of turning rivers into blood,
And caus'd their frogs and fnakes t' exift,
That with fome merit croak'd and hifs'd,
Yet ne'er by ev'ry quaint device,
Could frame the true Mofaic lice [154].
He for the Whigs his arts fhall try,
Their firft, and long their fole ally;
A patriot firm, while breath he draws,
He'll perifh in his country's caufe;

And

And when his magic labours ceafe,
Lie buried in eternal peace.

   Now view the fcenes in future hours,
That wait the famed European Pow'rs.
See where yon chalky cliffs arife,
The hills of Britain ftrike your eyes [155]:
Its fmall extenfion long fupplied,
By vaft immenfity of pride;
So small that had it found a ftation
In this new world at firft creation,
Or were by Juftice doom'd to fuffer,
And for its crimes tranfported over [156]
We'd find full room for't in lake Eri, or
That larger waterpond, Superior,
Where North on margin taking ftand,
Would not be able to fpy land [157].
No more, elate with pow'r, at eafe
She deals her infults round the feas;
See dwindling from her height amain,
What piles of ruin fpread the plain;
With mould'ring hulks her ports are fill'd,
And brambles clothe the cultur'd field!

                           See

See on her cliffs her Genius lies,
His handkerchief at both his eyes,
With many a deepdrawn sigh and groan,
To mourn her ruin and his own!
While joyous Holland, France and Spain,
With conq'ring navies rule the main,
And Ruffian banners wide unfurl'd,
Spread commerce round the eastern world [158].
And see (fight hateful and tormenting)
Th' Amer'can empire proud and vaunting,
From anarchy shall change her crasis,
And fix her pow'r on firmer basis;
To glory, wealth and fame ascend,
Her commerce rife, her realms extend;
Where now the panther guards his den,
Her defart forests swarm with men,
Her cities, tow'rs and columns rife,
And dazzling temples meet the skies;
Her pines descending to the main,
In triumph spread the watry plain,
Ride inland lakes with fav'ring gales,
And croud her ports with whit'ning fails;

Till

Till to the skirts of western day,
The peopled regions own her sway [159]."

Thus far M'Fingal told his tale,
When thundring shouts his ears assail,
And strait a Tory that stood centry,
Aghast rush'd headlong down the entry,
And with wild outcry, like magician,
Dispers'd the residue of vision [160]:
For now the Whigs intell'gence found
Of Tories mustring under ground,
And with rude bangs and loud uproar,
'Gan thunder furious at the door [161].
The lights put out, each Tory calls
To cover him, on cellar walls,
Creeps in each box, or bin, or tub,
To hide his head from wrath of mob,
Or lurks, where cabbages in row
Adorn'd the side with verdant show.
M'Fingal deem'd it vain to stay,
And risk his bones in second fray;
But chose a grand retreat from foes,
In lit'ral sense, beneath their nose [162].

The

The window then, which none else knew,
He softly open'd and crept thro'
And crawling flow in deadly fear,
By movements wife made good his rear.
Then scorning all the fame of martyr,
For Boston took his swift departure [162];
Nor dar'd look back on fatal spot,
More than the family of Lot [164].
Not North in more distress'd condition,
Outvoted first by opposition:
Nor good king George when that dire phantom
Of Independence comes to haunt him,
Which hov'ring round by night and day,
Not all his conj'rers yet can lay [165].
His friends, assembled for his sake,
He wisely left in pawn at stake,
To tarring, feath'ring, kicks and drubs
Of furious, disappointed mobs,
And with their forfeit hides to pay
For him, their leader, crept away [166].
So when wife Noah summon'd greeting
All animals to gen'ral meeting;

From

From ev'ry fide the members fent
All kinds of beafts to reprefent;
Each from the flood took care t' embark,
And fave his carcafe in the ark;
But as it fares in ftate and church,
Left his conftituents in the lurch.

FINIS.

NOTES.

CANTO I.

[1] The origin of the word Yankey (now spelled Yankee) is involved in obscurity. Some suppose it to be derived from an appellation in use in Europe, long before the settlement of the English colonies in America. Others, with more plausibility, say that it was coined from the guttural sound of the New England Indians in their attempt to pronounce the word *English*. The sound would be nearly represented thus—Yaunghees, the *g* being pronounced hard, and approaching to the sound of *k*, joined with a strong aspirate. The Dutch settlers on the Hudson adopted it as an epithet of derision, and applied it to all the inhabitants of New England. Dr. Thacher says that a farmer of Cambridge, Massachusetts, named Jonathan Hastings, who lived at about the year 1713, used it as a favorite cant word to express excellence, as a *yankee* good house, or *yankee* good cider. The students of Harvard on that account

called him *Yankee Jonathan*. As he was a weak man, when the students wished to denote a person of that character, they would call him *Yankee Jonathan*. It is now often used in England as a general name for the people of the United States. Layard, in his narrative of his discoveries at Nineveh, says that some of the natives there uttered a sound very similar to that of Yankee, in giving a general name to the Americans.

[2] This is in allusion to the tumultuous flight of the British toward Boston, after the skirmishes at Lexington and Concord on the 19th of April, 1775. It might also apply to many similar flights of the enemy during the war. This canto was published in the autumn of 1775, and the allusion was only to the events in the vicinity of Boston.

[3] When General Gage heard of the affair at Lexington, he sent out Lord Percy, a son of the Duke of Northumberland, with a reinforcement. Percy was a lineal descendant of the noted Earl Percy, who was slain in the battle of *Chevy Chase*, so celebrated in English song and story. As he marched out through Roxbury, his band playing Yankee Doodle, in derision, (it being then used in the British army as a sort of Rogue's March, when drumming delinquents out of the camp,) he observed a boy performing many antics. Percy asked him why he was so merry. "To think," said the shrewd lad, "how you will dance by-and-by, to *Chevy Chase*." Percy was often influenced

by presentiments, and the remark of the boy pressed heavily upon his spirits all the day.

⁴ M'Fingal is a representative of numerous magistrates at the commencement of the Revolution, who, desirous of retaining their offices, were over-zealous for the Crown, and became exceedingly obnoxious to the Whigs, as the Friends of Liberty were called.

⁵ Fingal was the Warrior King of ancient Scotland, celebrated for his martial deeds in the Poems of Ossian, a reputed Celtic Homer, who lived in the second or third century of the Christian Era. These poems, professedly translated from the Gælic, or Erse language, by James McPherson, a native of Inverness-shire, Scotland, were first published in 1762, under the title of *Fingal; An Ancient Epic Poem, in Six Books*. Many believe this epic to have been the offspring of the brain of McPherson alone. The question of its antiquity is yet open. McPherson was in America in 1770, as Surveyor General, under Governor Johnstone, of Florida; and it is asserted by McGregor, that he took his Gælic manuscripts with him, and lost many of them there.

⁶ The Gælic *Taischitaraugh*, a well-known Highland superstition. The belief was prevalent that certain persons were endowed with powers of divination, and that they would sometimes not only foretell events, but by some mysterious method, unknown to themselves had actual

visions of things distant, or in future. The belief was, according to Martin, universal in the Western Islands; and Dr. Johnson, in his narrative of his visit there, gives a graphic account of the superstition, and even defends it. Sir Walter Scott often used it with effect, in prose and verse. The character of M'Allister, in the *Legend of Montrose*, exhibits it; and in his fine ballad of *Lord Roland*, and in the *Lady of the Lake*, he has given glimpses of it. So has Campbell, in *Lochiel's Warning;* and Collins, in his ode on the *Superstitions of the Highlands* finely describes it. The belief has almost passed away, and now has existence only in tradition and poetry.

⁷ The English people had a traditional hatred of the Stuarts, which, after the rebellion in favor of the young Pretender, Charles Edward, in 1745, was extended, in a great degree, to the whole Scotch people. On the accession of George the Third, the minds of the English people, and especially of the ultra Protestants, were excited by unpleasant forebodings, because John, Earl of Bute, a needy Scotch adventurer, who had been the young King's tutor, was admitted to his counsels as Chief Minister, to the exclusion of the eminent William Pitt. He was a great favorite of the queen-dowager, and rumor spoke disparagingly of her virtue. These facts made the people fear the influence of the Jacobites, as the adherents of the Stuarts were called, in the affairs of

government; and somebody had the boldness, at the beginning of George's reign, to place a large placard on the Royal Exchange, with the words. "No Petticoat Government—No Scotch Minister." The Scotch were noted for their loyalty, in this country, and were generally found among the Tories, especially in the Carolinas. This fact, and the odium that rested upon the Jacobites in the mother country, made the Americans, during the Revolution, look with suspicion upon all Scotchmen. Jefferson manifested this feeling, when he drew up the Declaration of Independence. In the original draft, he alluded to "Scotch and foreign mercenaries." This was omitted, on motion of Dr. Witherspoon, who was a Scotchman by birth. In most minds, the word Jacobite was synonymous with Popery. Trumbull showed his dislike of the Scotch by his choice of a hero in this poem. Frenau, another eminent poet of the Revolution, also evinced the same hatred. In one of his poems, in which he gives Burgoyne many hard rubs, he consigns the Tories, with Burgoyne at their head, to an ice-bound, fog-covered island, off the northern coast of Scotland, thus:

> "There, Loyals, there, with loyal hearts, retire,
> There pitch your tents, and kindle there your fire;
> There desert Nature will her stings display,
> And fiercest hunger on your vitals prey;
> And with yourselves, let John Burgoyne retire,
> To reign your monarch, whom your hearts desire."

⁸ When bees are swarming, loud beating upon sonorous metal, such as tin pans, kettles, et cetera, causes them to alight, or "settle," when they are placed in a newly-prepared hive.

⁹ Alluding to the influences of the established churches of England and Scotland, in favor of the crown.

¹⁰ Bute is mentioned in a preceding note. Lord Mansfield, here alluded to, was a powerful supporter of the Ministry, and was employed to draw up many of the bills introduced after the passage of the famous stamp act, in 1765, for enslaving the colonies. On that account, and because of his Popish tendencies, he was hated by the Americans. He was one of the most able of the Chief Justices of England, and was raised to the peerage in 1776. Because he seemed to favor the Roman Catholics, his mansion was burned during the anti-Catholic riots in London in 1780, and with it his valuable collection of books and rare manuscripts.

¹¹ Soon after the accession of George the Third, Bute sent secret agents to America, to spy out the condition of the colonists. The Germans, who were then rapidly settling large districts in Pennsylvania, as well as in the Carolinas, were found to be a liberty-loving people, and generally inimical to royal prerogatives. The French Roman Catholics, then quite rapidly increasing in Maryland, and the French Protestants in South Carolina, were obnoxious to the same objections, and the

King was advised to cast obstacles in the way of emigration to the English colonies in America. Restrictive measures were soon employed, and a scheme was proposed to "reform the American Charters." In this lay the egg of active tyranny. This measure is alluded to in one of the charges made against the King in the Declaration of Independence.

[12] Sybillæ were prophetic women, ten in number, said to have lived in the early ages of Greece and Rome. The most noted of these was the Sybil of Cumæ, celebrated by Virgil in the sixth book of his *Æneid.* She is said to have written her prophecies in books, in which she foretold the fate of the Roman Empire. This Sybil was consulted by Æneas, and, according to the poets, she accompanied him to the lower world. She is probably the one who offered her books to Tarquin in his palace. She had nine volumes, which she offered to sell to Tarquin at a very high price. He refused. She disappeared, burned three of them, and then offered him the remaining six at the same price. He again refused, when she burned three more, and came on the same errand. The astonished Emperor bought the remaining three, and they were long preserved with the greatest care. The whole story is probably a poetic fable, covering some important fact in Roman history.

[13] Dodona was the most ancient oracle in Greece and is said to have been consulted by the Pelasgi.

The responses of the oracle were delivered by a priestess, from the sacred oak or beach. There were two oracles of the same name, one at Epirus, and one in Thessaly.

[14] The tripod was an ancient three-legged stool, on which priests and priestesses sat when they uttered their oracles.

[15] In the autumn of 1775, the British government bargained with some of the petty German princes for about seventeen thousand troops, to assist in crushing the rebellion in America. As the larger portion of these troops were hired from the Prince of Hesse Cassel, they bore the general name of *Hessians*, and as such are known in the history of our War for Independence. They came in the summer and autumn of 1776, and were first let loose upon the patriots on Long Island, and in lower Westchester County, New York. They were generally ignorant, bloodthirsty and cruel, and were despised by the English soldiers. They were employed in the least honorable enterprises during the war, especially in forays upon hamlets, and the burning of towns. They cost the British government a million of dollars, and a vast amount of reputation among the nations. The scheme for their employment was distasteful even to the King, and it was denounced in Parliament, as "disgraceful to the British name."

[16] This prophecy was but half accomplished

The mercenaries did come over, but the hanging, and division of estates never occurred.

[17] A Grecian warrior and herald, in the army that besieged Troy. His voice, according to Homer, was louder than the combined voices of fifty men.

[18] In the wars between the ancient Greeks and Persians, and other eastern nations, elephants were employed. Sometimes they became frightened, turned and fled. In their flight they would trample upon those " they came to aid."

[19] Penelope, wife of Ulysses, monarch of Ithaca, who was remarkable for her fidelity to her husband. Ulysses was absent twenty years, after his departure for the siege of Troy. Many lovers sought the hand of Penelope, and her relatives urged her to abandon all thoughts of her husband's return. She finally agreed to make choice of one of the suitors as soon as she should complete a web she was then weaving, as a funeral ornament for the aged Laertes. Every night she would undo all that she had wrought in the day time, and thus she protracted her promise until the final return of her husband.

[20] The British Parliament, in its assertion of its power "to bind the colonies in all cases whatsoever," levied a small duty upon all tea imported into the colonies. The sum was small, but the *principles* involved were of vast importance. The colonists had already stoutly opposed govern-

ment measures having a like tendency to tax the people without their consent, and had boldly enunciated the grand postulate, that TAXATION WITHOUT REPRESENTATION, IS OPPRESSION. The even nominal duty on tea, levied without the consent of the colonists, was in violation of the freedom negatively asserted in that postulate, and the people resolved not to submit to the tax. They held meetings, declared that tea should not be landed for sale on our shores, while the duty remained, warned consignees not to offend the popular will, and appointed committees of vigilance and correspondence to see that that will had free exercise. Commotions ensued, cargoes of tea were destroyed, and the Revolutionary crisis was thus hastened. For ten long years, the people had remonstrated, petitioned, addressed the King, Parliament and people of Great Britain, but to no purpose, and so, despairing of redress, and determined to be free, they raised the arm of resistance, and the war began.

[21] The terms Whig and Tory were adopted at an early period of the struggle. The appellation of Tory was first given to the wild Irish, outside of the English real jurisdiction in Ireland, who made predatory war against the British settlements in Dublin and vicinity. In the civil wars in the reign of Charles the First, these clans adhered to the royal party. The name was also applied to a volunteer troop of cavalry in Charles's

army, composed of young noblemen, and the sons of gentlemen, who were famous for revelry, and the singing of songs, the chorus of which consisted in a roll of unmeaning words. They had a favorite ballad, suited to the times, the chorus of which was,

"Sing *tory*, rory, rantum, sanctum, tory rory row."

The origin of the word Whig is not so clear. Some say that it originally meant a sour kind of crab-apple, and that it was applied to the Puritans in the army of Cromwell, who clipped their hair short, scowled upon all pleasantries, &c. They were called Whigs, prick-ears, and roundheads. Bishop Burnet gives a different account of its origin. The waggoners in the West of Scotland, when driving their horses, used the word *whiggam*, and the drivers were called *whiggamores*, abbreviated to whiggs. On one occasion, about six thousand of these people marched to Edinburgh, headed by the Marquis of Argyle, to oppose the ministerial troops, and, after that, all who opposed the court, were called Whigs, in contempt. Ever since then, the court party in England have been called Tories, and their opponents Whigs. These were significant terms for the Americans at the commencement of the revolutionary contest, and became common in 1774.

[22] Allusion is here probably made to a King of the Averni district whom Cæsar made a prisoner after his last battle with and final conquest of the

Gauls, and carried in triumph to Rome. When he laid the royal ensigns and arms at the foot of Cæsar, he exclaimed. " Receive them ; thou, O, bravest of men, hast conquered a brave man." The Senate decreed a triumph to Cæsar, and the Gallic King and other notable prisoners were astonished and awed by the great display of wealth, and power, and pageantry, in the imperial city.

[23] Formerly town meetings were usually held in the churches or meeting-houses in the country towns of New England.

[24] Mercury was the messenger of the gods, and is represented with wings upon his cap and feet, and bearing a staff (caduceus) in his hand, about which serpents are entwined. Mercury was also considered the patron of eloquence, and of thieves, and other dishonest persons.

[25] In many parts of New England, the term *Moderator* is yet given to the chairman of the meeting, whether political or religious. In the present case, he is seated in one of those high, old-fashioned pulpits, which seemed to have been constructed chiefly for the purpose of concealing the person of the speaker.

[26] During the summer and autumn of 1774, the people of the colonies, especially those of New England, commenced arming themselves. They practised daily in military exercises ; the manufacture of gunpowder was encouraged ; and throughout Massachusetts in particular, the people were en-

rolled as a militia force, in companies, prepared to take up arms, and rush to the field at a minute's warning. From this circumstance, they were called *minute-men.* Such were the men who opposed the British at Lexington and Concord, and annoyed them by a galling fire from behind hedges and stone walls, all the way of their retreat to Boston.

[27] Æolus was the god or ruler of the winds; and was represented as holding them in restraint, in a great cave, from which they issued at his bidding.

[28] Numbers, chapter xii.

[29] Honorius, as opposed to M'Fingal, is a representative of a stanch Whig patriot, and a bold leader of his class.

[30] British statesmen, opposed to the colonists, in their struggle for freedom, were fond of boasting of the *liberality* of Great Britain, toward her children in the New World. They were either ignorant of, or artfully concealed the fact, that England had been fully repaid for all her boasted aids, by services, the most arduous and important. All of the settlements, except Georgia, had been made on private account; and all through the colonial period, the connection with Great Britain was a detriment to the colonies, rather than a benefit. For long and gloomy years, they had struggled up, from feebleness to strength, unaided and alone. They had built fortifications, raised armies, and fought battles, for England's glory

and their own preservation, without England's aid, and often without her sympathy. In 1758 when the French and Indian War was progressing, public and private advances to carry on the war, made in Massachusetts alone, amounted to more than a million of dollars. The taxes on real estate, in order to raise money, were enormous; in many instances, equal to two-thirds of the income of the tax-payers. Yet it was levied by *their own representatives*, and they did not complain. Lord Baltimore spent £200,000 sterling, in colonizing Maryland; and William Penn became deeply involved in debt, in his efforts to settle and improve Pennsylvania. On one occasion, in 1765, Charles Townshend, in the House of Commons, spoke of the Americans as children planted by the care of Great Britain, nourished up by its indulgence, and protected by its arms. Colonel Barre replied, " They *planted by your care!* No, your *oppressions* planted them in America." * * * " They *nourished up by your indulgence!* They grew by your *neglect* of them." * * * * * " They *protected by your arms!* They have nobly taken up arms in your defence." And then he recounted the valorous deeds of the Americans, and warned the English legislature that " that same spirit of freedom which actuated the people at first," in fleeing from persecution, would " accompany them still," and predicted that they would take up arms in defence of their liberties

[31] Growth and decay seem to be the law of progress in nations as well as individuals. This truth, all past history teaches us. States have their youth, maturity, and season of decrepitude before decay.

[31] This is to become a public charge. The national debt of England, at that time, was more than seven hundred and fifty millions of dollars. The debt was commenced by William the Third, and the English people were alarmed at its amount, in 1697, then only twenty-five millions of dollars. At the close of the war of the Revolution, in 1783, it had swelled to about thirteen hundred millions. Now (1857) it is more than four thousand millions of dollars!

[33] This alludes to the time of the elder Pitt's administration, when Canada was wrested from the French, and a vast empire in India lay prostrate at the feet of Great Britain. Fifteen years had now elapsed, and the Gallic or French power had loomed up amazingly, and the traditionary feud between the two people, though quieted by treaties, was as fierce as ever. When our Revolution broke out, the French perceived an opportunity to damage England, by helping her rebellious colonies. Early in the struggle, the Americans received material aid from France, and finally, in 1778, formed a treaty of alliance with that nation. For three years, Gallic crows had been whetting " their beaks to pick her."

[34] An ancient "Hospital of St. Mary of Bethlehem," situated in London, and incorporated by Henry the Eighth, in 1546. The hospital building in Moorfields, which was erected in 1675, was pulled down in 1814. The present buildings of the institution are in St. George's Fields. It has long been used as a hospital for lunatics, which explains the allusion in the poem. In later editions of this poem, the word Bethlehem is changed to *Bedlam*. The latter is a corruption of the former.

[35] "Who sees thee? (and what is one?) who shouldst
   be seen,
A goddess among gods, adored and served,
By angels numberless thy daily train."
                              Satan to Eve.

*   *   *   *   *   *   *

            —"but henceforth my early care,
Not without song, each morning and due praise,
Shall tend thee, and the fertile burden ease
Of thy full branches, offered free to all;
Till, dieted by thee, I grow mature
In knowledge as the gods, who all things know."
Eve to the Tree of Life, Milton's Paradise Lost, Book IX.

[36] Special reference is here made to an act, passed by the British Parliament in 1766, known as the *Declaratory Act*, in which the omnipotence of the British Parliament was affirmed, and its "right" declared to bind the colonies in all cases whatsoever." This measure, strange as it may appear, was proposed by Pitt, who had

labored zealously for the repeal of the odious stamp act. It was a necessary expedient, he thought, in order to insure that repeal, but it unfortunately became the egg from which issued the most obnoxious measures.

³⁷ When, in 1534, Henry the Eighth of England quarrelled with the Pope, he cast off his allegiance to the Pontiff, and settled the supremacy over the Church and State, in his dominions, in the person of the Sovereign. The monarchs of England have ever since asserted and maintained that supremacy.

³⁸ It is asserted (and positively denied) that, in the ninth century, a female named Joan conceived a violent passion for a young monk named Felda, and in order to be admitted into his monastery, assumed the garb of a man. On the death of her lover, she entered upon the duties of Professor, and, being very learned, was elected Pope on the death of Adrian, in 872. This story has occasioned violent disputes among ecclesiastical historians. We have no record of any trial to prove her sex, as in the case of the Chevalier D'Eon, before Lord Mansfield.

³⁹ The English Parliament House is called St. Stephen's Chapel. A chapel so called in honor of Stephen, the proto-martyr, was erected by King Stephen, at about the year 1135. It was rebuilt in 1347, and about the year 1550, it was applied to the use of Parliament.

[40] Lord North, Earl of Guilford, became First Lord of the Treasury, or Prime Minister of England, in 1770, and continued in that important office until 1782. He was a well-meaning man, but lacked the better qualities of a great statesman; and by his official blunders, obstinacy, and unwise measures, he was chiefly instrumental in alienating the loyalty of the American people, and in causing and protracting their armed struggle for independence. He was blind for some years before his death, which occurred in July, 1792, when he was sixty years of age. See note 157, Canto IV.

[41] This is in allusion to the measure known as the *Quebec Act*, in the spring of 1774, which established the Roman Catholic religion in Canada. When the British ministry perceived the general disaffection in the American colonies, and the probability that the important province of Canada would join in the revolt, this conciliatory measure toward the Roman Catholic population there, was intended to prevent such a result. The cry of "No Popery" was then very popular in England, and the Quebec Act deeply offended public sentiment there, and in America. The title here given to the central Papal authority is derived from the 17th chapter of *Revelations*.

[42] At the commencement of hostilities, British ships and armies were employed in plundering our seas, ravaging our coast, burning our towns, and

destroying the lives of our people, and when, in the summer of 1779, the royal Governor of New York, William Tryon, had burned East Haven, Fairfield, and Norwalk, in Connecticut, on Long Island Sound, and openly insulted the defenceless inhabitants, he boasted of his extreme *leniency* in leaving a single house standing on the New England coast. And British *ministers* often disgusted their own people by repeating that boast.

[43] One of the great foundations of the British Constitution was obtained from Charles the First by Parliament, in 1628, by his signature to a bill which recognized all the legal privileges of the subject. On the accession of William and Mary, in 1689, a *Bill of Rights*, declaratory of the franchises of British subjects, was passed, and received the royal signature. It is the only *written law* respecting the liberties of the British people, except MAGNA CHARTA—the Great Charter.

[44] For ten long years, the colonists petitioned the King and Parliament for justice, and a redress of grievances. Instead of listening and complying, the government denied their prayer, sometimes with indifference, at others with insults, and again by an accumulation of oppressive measures, which restricted personal liberty and commercial operations.

[45] First Kings, chapter xviii. Baal, or Belus, was the chief idol among the idolatrous nations of Canaan and vicinity.

[46] The crocodile was worshipped in only some portions of Ancient Egypt; in others it was warred upon; and the ichneumon, which destroyed its eggs, was regarded with great favor. Many mummied crocodiles have been found at Thebes, and at the modern Maahdah, where extensive grottos contain them. Persons were sometimes eaten by the beast, after having adored it.

[47] In almost every speech from the throne, concerning the American people, the King used honeyed words, and the colonists were often deceived by false hopes, springing from the promises of "His Most *Gracious* Majesty," which ministers compelled him to break. The hopes which budded in the warmth of these promises, were uniformly blasted by the frosts of Parliamentary action.

[48] In consequence of the destruction of tea in Boston Harbor, [see note 31, p. 257,] and other overt acts of rebellion, so called, Parliament, by enactment in the spring of 1774, ordered the port of Boston to be closed against all shipping, and suspended all commercial operations there. This is known as the Boston Port Bill, which was productive of more real misery, and greater irritation, than any other of the obnoxious measures of the ministry. Soon after the passage of that bill, others, equally tyrannical, were adopted. Among them was one, whose operations were equivalent to a total subversion of the Charter of Massa-

chusetts. Other colonies were threatened with a similar lash, if they dared to raise voice or hand against the omnipotence of Parliament. By that enactment, every thing pertaining to courts of law and equity was placed in the hands of the creatures of the government; and the officers in the province were made independent of the people by receiving their salaries from the crown.

[49] Thomas Gage was a native of England, and was an active officer during the French and Indian War. He was appointed Military Governor of Montreal in 1760, and on the departure of Amherst from America in 1763, he succeeded that officer as Commander-in-chief of the British forces in America. He was appointed Governor of Massachusetts, in the place of Hutchinson, in 1774, and went to Boston on the first of June, fully authorized and prepared to enforce the provisions of the Port Bill, by arms if necessary. He was naturally amiable in disposition, but in executing the will of his royal master, he became, necessarily, a tyrant. Gage was the last royal Governor of Massachusetts. Howe succeeded him as military commander in the summer of 1775, and he went to England in the autumn of the same year, where he died in April, 1787.

[50] This is a law term, signifying "the power of the country," or the citizens who are summoned to assist an officer in suppressing a riot, or in executing any legal precept which is forcibly opposed.

⁵¹ Genesis, chapter iii.

—" In at his mouth
The devil entered, and his brutal sense
In heart or head, possessing, soon inspired
With act intelligential."
Paradise Lost, Book IX.

⁵² A writ of ejectment.

⁵³ At the commencement of the contest, loyalists and timid republicans, desirous of conciliating government officers, formally *addressed* them, and assured them of friendship and support. In Boston, in 1774, when General Gage was enforcing the Port Bill with rigor, one hundred and twenty merchants and others, signed an address to Gage, expressive of their gratitude and loyalty, and even went so far as to offer to pay the East India Company for the tea destroyed in December previous. There were some others who *protested* against the course of the Committee of Correspondence, and the action of a large portion of the ministers of the Gospel in New England, who, they averred, were unduly exciting the people, and urging them to ruin. These "Addressors and Protestors" were summarily dealt with by the Whigs, and many of them were compelled to sign a recantation which the General Committee of Correspondence for Massachusetts declared satisfactory. Those who would not sign it left the province, and became the first Refugee Royal-

ists. See Lossing's Pictorial Field Book of the Revolution, i., 512.

[54] At the commencement of the war, great prejudice prevailed throughout most of the colonies, and especially in New England, against the clergy, and even many of the laity of the Church of England, as the Protestant Episcopal Church was called. There were many reasons for this prejudice. For a long time Archbishop Secker and others had labored zealously in efforts to establish Episcopacy in America, which the colonists regarded as ano her form of oppression, because it was so intimately connected with the throne; so they strenuously resisted such efforts. Sometimes newspaper and pamphlet controversies on the subject ran high, and were very bitter. Cooper, of King's College, Auchmuty, Chandler, and other Episcopal clergymen, kept their pens quite actively engaged, while William Livingston, of New Jersey, was equally active with his pen, in opposition. The Church clergy constantly harped upon, and were in favor of the absurd doctrines of passive obedience, non-resistance, and the divine right of Kings, and were active in endeavors to produce divisions among the patriots. The fact that for several years previous to the Revolution, the whole bench of Bishops, in the British Parliament, were opposed to the colonists, and always advised coercive measures, made their class obnoxious to the patriots. Again, the Episcopal clergy gener-

ally took sides with the Crown, and joined in the hue and cry against the leading Whigs. One of their writers, in Hugh Gaine's New York Mercury, in 1768, supposed to have been Dr. Auchmuty, of Trinity Church, or Professor Vardell, of King's College, thus alluded to Livingston, in a long poem. It must be remembered that Livingston wrote anonymously:

> "Some think him a *Tindall*, some think him a *Chubb*,
> Some think him a *Ranter*, that sports from his tub;
> Some think him a *Newton*, some think him a *Locke*,
> Some think him a *Stone*, some think him a *Stock*.
> But a *Stock* he at least may thank Nature for giving,
> And if he's a STONE, I pronounce it a LIVING."

[15] The stories of the wonderful exploits of St. Anthony and his pigs, and of St. Austin preaching to the fishes, are told in the Popish legends.

[16] William Walter, D. D., was rector of Trinity Church, Summer street, Boston. He was placed over that congregation in 1768, and left his people early in 1776, after this canto of M'Fingal was written. He was an addressor of Gage, and was among the proscribed and banished. He was afterwards Chaplain to De Lancey's Third Battalion of American Loyalists, and at the close of the war he went to Nova Scotia, and took charge of a church at Shelburne. He died at Boston, in the year 1800. Before he left his flock in Boston, he preached many furious discourses against rebellion, and often warned his people of

the dangers of the halter that awaited those who lifted their hands against "the powers that be."

⁵⁷ Samuel Auchmuty, D. D., was the son of an eminent lawyer and Judge of Admiralty, in Massachusetts. He was a graduate of Harvard College, and received his Doctorate of Divinity from Oxford, England. He was chosen rector of Trinity Church, in New York, on the death of Dr. Barclay, in 1764, and continued his connection until the summer of 1776, when, with his family, he retired to New Jersey. He died the following spring. His sermons, before the breaking out of the war, were strongly denunciatory of the Sons of Liberty, as the associated patriots were called, the most prominent of whom, in New York, was Isaac Sears, (commonly known as "King Sears,") who was a member of his church, and at the close of the war, was a vestryman. In April, 1775, Dr. Auchmuty wrote from New York to Captain Montressor, Gage's Chief Engineer in Boston: "We have lately been plagued with a rascally Whig mob here, but they have effected nothing, only Sears, the King, was rescued at the jail door. [See note 69] * * * Our magistrates have not the spirit of a louse."

⁵⁸ Samuel Peters, D. D., was a native of Hebron, Connecticut, a graduate of Yale College, and a Tory Episcopal clergyman. His loyalty and his lack of judgment led him into many difficulties, and he became exceedingly obnoxious to the

Whigs. He was compelled to sign retractions and declarations, but, finding Hebron too hot for him, he fled to Boston, and took shelter under the British flag. He seems to have indulged a peculiar spite against his native State, and proposed a scheme for wiping it off the list of Commonwealths, partitioning it between New York and Massachusetts. He went to England, and remained abroad until 1805, when he returned to America. In the meanwhile, he was elected Bishop of Vermont, but declined the honor. He had also written a History of Connecticut, which is a contemptible libel, and full of untruths. He never acknowledged being the author, but the fact is well known. In the years 1817 and 1818, he journeyed to the far North West, even to the Falls of St. Anthony. He died at New York on the 19th of April, 1826, aged 90 years, and was buried at Hebron.

[59] Myles Cooper, D. D., was President of King's (now Columbia) College, at the commencement of the Revolution, and for some years previous. He was educated at Oxford, England, came to America in 1762, and the next year was made President of the College. His opposition to the patriots was violent and unrelenting, yet some of the students under his care, among whom was Alexander Hamilton, boldly defied his menaces. He became very obnoxious to the Whigs; and, finally, feeling alarmed for his personal safety, he fled in haste

from the College, took refuge in Stuyvesant's house, near the East River, and made his escape. on board the *Asia,* a British man-of-war. He went to England soon afterward, and never returned. He died suddenly at Edinburgh, in 1785, at the age of fifty years. Among his papers was found the following epitaph, written by himself:

"Here lies a priest of English blood,
Who, living, liked whate'er was good;
Good company, good wine, good name,
Yet never hunted after fame."

"Samuel Seabury, D. D., was the first Bishop of the Protestant Episcopal Church in America. He was a native of New London, Connecticut, where his remains were laid at death. He took orders in the Church in London, in 1753, and became pastor of a congregation in New Brunswick, New Jersey. He afterwards took charge of a small flock at Jamaica, Long Island, and from there he went to Westchester county, New York, where he was settled at the commencement of the Revolution. There he took an active part with the loyalists, and was one of a large number who met at White Plains, and signed a protest against "all unlawful Congresses and Committees," and expressed their determination "to support the King and Constitution," at all hazards. These proceedings made him a mark for public indignation, and when, in the autumn of 1775, a party of

light horsemen from Connecticut, led by "King
Sears," returned from destroying Rivington's
printing press in New York, they carried Mr.
Seabury with them as a prisoner to Connecticut.
After his release, he became Chaplain in Colonel
Fanning's American Regiment of Loyalists. He
settled at New London, at the close of the war;
was consecrated bishop in Scotland in 1784, and
presided over the dioceses of Connecticut and
Rhode Island, until his death, in February, 1796.
He was highly esteemed for his piety and learning.

[61] Judges, chapter v.

[62] Revelations, chapter xiii.

[63] A kind of paste-blacking, containing grease, and much used in those days for the preservation of shoes from the effects of water. It was made in the form of a ball.

[64] A soft, friable clay, which absorbs grease, and was much used in fulling cloth.

[65] In allusion to the sale of Indulgences in the Papal Church, by which, for certain sums of money, a man was allowed to commit certain sins, and even great crimes. This practice was commenced by Pope Leo the Third, about the year 800. Urban used them for revenue in 1090, and afterwards they were offered by the Roman Pontiffs as awards to the Crusaders. Clement the First made the first public sale of them in 1313. In 1517, Leo the Tenth published general Indul-

gences throughout Europe, and this great socia.
grievance led to the Reformation, first in Germany, and then in England, in 1534. They were pardon for sins past, present, and future; and were written upon parchment, and signed by the Pope or his legates.

⁶⁶ 1 Samuel, chapter x.

⁶⁷ This refers to the position of the Pope of Rome, who is also a temporal prince.

⁶⁸ See Virgil's *Æneid*, book vi.

⁶⁹ James Rivington, printer of the *Royal Gazette*, in New York, during the Revolution. He came to America from London, in 1760, established a bookstore, first in Philadelphia, and then in New York, and in 1773 commenced his paper, first called the *Royal Gazetteer*. No man was more detested by the Whigs than Rivington, and his paper received the name of the *Lying Gazette*. Frenau, another poet of the Revolution, gave him many hard blows; and at public meetings he was everywhere denounced. In the autumn of 1775 a party of light horsemen from Connecticut, led by Isaac Sears, (one of the chiefs of the Sons of Liberty in New York,) rode into the city, dismounted in front of Rivington's printing office, and deliberately destroyed his press, and carried off his types. The following year, when the British had taken possession of New York, he was appointed King's Printer, resumed the publication of his paper, and continued it until the

close of the war, when, to the astonishment of all, he remained in the city unmolested, while far less sinful loyalists felt compelled to flee to Canada and Nova Scotia. The reason is in the fact, that he was false to his royal master, and that during the latter years of the war, while he was abusing the Whigs the most, he was secretly conveying intelligence to General Washington of all the important movements of the British in the city. See Lossing's Pictorial Field Book of the Revolution, ii., 591. Rivington died in New York in July, 1802, at the age of seventy-eight years.

⁷⁰ Crean Brush was a conceited and sycophantic loyalist in New York. He was a native of Cumberland county, (now forming a part of the southern portion of Vermont, next to New York,) and member of the Assembly. In February, 1775, he made a speech against the appointment of delegates to the second Continental Congress, which was published. It was answered by Philip Schuyler and George Clinton. He continually opposed Whig measures; and after the battle of Bunker Hill, we find him in Boston, ready, with supple muscles, to do the will of General Howe, in damaging the patriots.

⁷¹ Dr. Myles Cooper, referred to in note 59.

⁷² Isaac Wilkins, D. D., was the son of a rich West India planter, and when quite young was sent to New York to be educated. He prepared himself for the ministry, but did not take orders

until some years afterward. He settled in Westchester county, became a member of the New York Assembly, and was considered a leader on the ministerial side. He had great influence, and chiefly through his instrumentality, a resolution to pass a vote of thanks to the New York Delegates to the Continental Congress, offered by the early martyr, Nathaniel Woodhull, was lost. His speech in opposition to the appointment of Delegates to the Second Continental Congress, is preserved in Sabine's *Lives of the American Loyalists*. He was very obnoxious to the Whigs, and young Alexander Hamilton became his opponent with the pen. Wilkins soon abandoned the county, went to England, but returned to Long Island in 1776. There he remained until the end of the war, when he retired to Shelburne, in Nova Scotia. In the meanwhile he had taken orders in the Church; and in the year 1800, he became rector of an Episcopal parish in Westchester county, where he continued in the ministry until his death, in 1830, at the age of eighty-nine years.

[73] Samuel Chandler was a High Church clergyman, in New York, and was one of the earliest in that city to denounce the measures of the Sons of Liberty. He became very obnoxious to the Whigs, and in 1775, he went to England, and never returned.

[74] Benjamin Booth was a stanch loyalist, and was for a time Secretary of the Loyal Refugees

of the different colonies, whose head-quarters were in New York, under the protection of British arms. He called a meeting of the loyalists in that city in September, 1778, when, it appears, about two thousand of them were present.

[75] A series of well-written essays, against Whig measures, over the signature of "Massachusettensis," were published in Boston papers, between December, 1774, and April, 1775. The authorship was long attributed to Jonathan Sewall, but they were really the production of Daniel Leonard, of Taunton, Massachusetts, who was one of the Mandamus Council. [See note 85]. Leonard was a graduate of Harvard College, was bred to the law, and became an acute logician, and powerful political writer. He was a member of the General Court of Massachusetts, and was one of the barristers, who, in 1774, signed an address to Governor Hutchinson. Bullets were fired into his house by a mob, and he took refuge in Boston in May, 1775. In 1776 he accompanied the British army to Halifax, and afterward became Chief Justice of the Bermudas. He died in London in 1829, at the age of eighty-nine years. His essays, above alluded to, were answered by John Adams, over the signature of "Novanglus," in a series published between January and the 19th of April, 1775. Both were reprinted in 1819 with a preface by Mr. Adams.

[76] Those powerful and widely-scattered engines

of the Revolution, *Committees of Correspondence* became exceedingly hateful to the government and the loyalists. Massachusetts and Virginia have disputed the honor of originating them. They seem to have been conceived by leading patriots almost simultaneously in both colonies, in 1773, and in 1774; they existed all over the land. They were the depositories and distributors of secret information of every kind, and through them, concert of political action was seen every where, from New Hampshire to Georgia. Of these " Massachusettensis " said, " This is the foulest, subtlest, and most venomous serpent ever issued from the egg of sedition. *It is the source of the rebellion.* I saw the small seed when it was implanted; [by Samuel Adams] it was a grain of mustard. I have watched the plant until it has become a great tree. The vilest reptiles that crawl upon the earth are concealed at the root; the foulest birds of the air rest upon its branches. I now would induce you to go to work immediately with axes and hatchets to cut it down, for a twofold reason; because it is a pest to society, and lest it be felled suddenly, by a stronger arm, and crush its thousands in its fall."

[77] Thomas Hutchinson, Governor of Massachusetts, from 1771 until superseded by Gage, in the spring of 1774. He was a native of that province, held many important public offices, and wrote a valuable history of his native colony. Some of his

obnoxious acts will be referred to hereafter. He became alarmed for his personal safety, and fled to England. The allusion of the poet is to a laudatory address which loyalists and timid Whigs presented to him, just before his departure. He died in England in June, 1789.

[78] Jonathan Sewall was a native of Massachusetts, was educated at Harvard College, became a school teacher, and then a lawyer, and at about the year 1767, was appointed Attorney-General of Massachusetts. It is believed that he was disposed to take part with the Whigs, but had not the courage. He and John Adams were intimate friends, and that friendship was not broken, even after Sewall became one of the addressors of Hutchinson in 1774. Later in the season, he tried to persuade Adams not to attend the Continental Congress, when the firm patriot used those remarkable words: "The die is now cast; I have now passed the Rubicon; swim or sink, live or die survive or perish, with my country, is my unalterable determination." They never met again until after the war. Judge Sewall became Gage's chief adviser, and, it is said, wrote most of his proclamations. He was an essayist of some distinction. His house at Cambridge was attacked by a mob, and he fled to Boston; and in 1775 he went to England, and resided at Bristol. In 1788, he came to America, and was made Judge of Admiralty in the province of New Brunswick

He died there in 1796, at the age of sixty-eight years. His wife was a sister of Dorothy Quincy, wife of John Hancock.

[79] Nathaniel Mills and John Hicks were printers of a ministerial paper in Boston. They opened a printing-house, as partners, in School street, in 1773, and their paper, the *Massachusetts Gazette and Boston Post Boy*, became the government organ in that city. The commencement of hostilities, in 1775, put an end to their paper, and the following spring they accompanied the refugee loyalists who fled to Halifax with the British army, when Washington drove it out of Boston. They afterwards opened a stationery store in New York, and printed some for the royal army and navy. They were among the New York refugees who fled to Nova Scotia, at the close of the war.

[80] Margaret, was the widow of Richard Draper, printer of the *Massachusetts Gazette and News Letter*, who died in Boston, in June, 1774. Mrs. Draper continued the paper after the death of her husband. She became his successor as printer to the Governor and Council, and continued business while the British were in possession of Boston. It was the first and the last newspaper published in Boston, previous to the Declaration of Independence. Mrs. Draper went to Halifax with the army, and from thence accompanied friends to England, where she received a pension until her death, a few years afterward.

[81] Judge Sewall wrote a farce called *America Arouse*. It was a dull affair—a farce of itself, and not to be laughed at.

[82] The oppressive provisions of the Boston Port Bill, went into effect on the first of June, 1774. The Provincial Congress of Massachusetts appointed that day as one of solemn fasting and prayer, for the people of the province.

[83] In various places the people had signed a League, agreeing not to import or use tea in any way, while a duty levied by government without the consent of the colonists, remained upon that article. Yet men were found among loyalists bold enough to brave public opinion by becoming consignees. Intelligence reached America that ships laden with tea were crossing the ocean. The people gathered, and made preparations in several seaport towns to prevent the landing of the cargoes. Two tea ships arrived in Boston, late in 1773. The consignees were warned of danger, but refused to listen. They were threatened by mobs; and one of them, Richard Clarke, had his house damaged by missles thrown by a crowd of excited people. Finally, on the evening of the 16th of December, a party, many of them disguised, went on board the tea ships, and cast their contents into Boston Harbor. The consignees were despised as supple tools of the British ministry, and this popular demonstration

kept them quiet and inactive ever afterward. See note 31, Canto iii.

[84] Peter Oliver, a native of Massachusetts, was made, first a Judge of the Superior Court, and then Chief Justice of the province, notwithstanding he was not bred a lawyer, nor possessed a knowledge of legal science. He was graduated at Harvard in 1730, and possessed some learning and fair abilities, but was totally unfit for the high office which he held. Because he received his salary direct from the crown, instead of the people of Massachusetts, and thus became independent of the latter, he was impeached in 1774, and soon afterward went to England. He died at Birmingham, in the autumn of 1791.

[85] A writ of mandamus is a command from a high power, to any person, corporation, or inferior court, requiring them to do some specified act which appertains to their office or duty. By the charter of Massachusetts, the Council had always been elective, but by one of the bills passed by Parliament in the spring of 1774, that charter was declared void, and the King appointed a council by mandamus. They were, of course, chosen from among the loyalists, and many of them accepted the office, and took the prescribed oath. These councillors became very detestable to the Whigs, who regarded their act as equivalent to joining the crown in its oppressions.

⁵⁶ "A proper emblem of his genius," says Trumbull.

⁵⁷ John Murray was a native of Rutland, in Massachusetts, a colonel of militia, and for several years a member of the General Court. He was one of the Mandamus Council, but was not sworn into office. Menaced by the Whigs, he abandoned his house in the night, fled to Boston, and accompanied the British army to Halifax in 1776. After the war, Colonel Murray became a resident of St. Johns, New Brunswick. His large property in the United States was confiscated, yet he left a handsome estate in St. Johns.

⁵⁸ Timothy Ruggles was an old stager in public life, having been a member of the Massachusetts Assembly as early as 1736. He was a man of decided talents and energy, a lawyer by profession, but for many years was a tavern-keeper in Sandwich. He loved military life, attained to the rank of a brigadier-general, and led a body of troops to join Sir William Johnson, in 1755. He was distinguished in the battle at the head of Lake George that year. Two years afterward, he was appointed a Judge; and in 1765, he was one of the Massachusetts delegates to the "Stamp Act Congress," assembled at New York. He was President of that body, but his conduct was so loyal toward the crown, that he was censured by the Assembly of his province. When the Revolution broke out, he was a violent opponent of the Whigs, and

crowned his detested acts by becoming a Mandamus Councillor. His house was attacked, his cattle were injured, and in terror, he fled to Boston, and endeavored to raise a volunteer corps of loyalists. He then proposed associations to act against the Whigs; and when the British army fled to Halifax, he was among the refugee loyalists who accompanied it. He afterwards appeared upon Long Island and Staten Island, and succeeded in raising a military corps of about three hundred men, called the *Loyal Militia*, but he did not perform much service with them. His property was confiscated in 1779, and he went to Nova Scotia at the conclusion of the war. He died in 1798 at the age of eighty-seven years. Mercy Warren, in her drama called *The Group*, gives him the character of *Hate-all*, because he was a sort of social Ishmael.

⁶⁹ Josiah Edson, of Bridgewater, Massachusetts, was an active politician, and was known by the odious names of Rescinder and Mandamus Councillor. He was a man of weak courage, and was rather a passive than an active loyalist, yet a mob attacked his house, and he was compelled to flee to Boston for safety, in 1774. He went to Halifax in 1776, and afterwards became a resident in the city (or its vicinity) of New York, where he died. He is represented as an amiable, virtuous and highly respectable man. But mobs make no distinction of persons, if their avowed *principles* are offensive.

[90] Nathaniel Ray Thomas was a resident of Marshfield, and a graduate of Harvard University in 1751. Having become a member of the Mandamus Council, he shared in the afflictions of that unhappy body, who seemed to receive the special attention of mobs. He went to Halifax in 1776, and in 1778 his property was confiscated. He died in Nova Scotia in 1791.

[91] This was Joshua Loring, of Massachusetts, whose property was confiscated, and himself banished. He became British commissary of prisoners in Boston, and is charged with the perpetration of most outrageous cruelties toward them. It is affirmed that when he fled to England, his wife did not accompany him, but remained as mistress of General Sir William Howe. An allusion is made to her in Francis Hopkinson's *Battle of the Kegs*, as " Mrs. L——g." Loring left behind him a name most odious, and he never returned to America. He died in England, in 1782.

[92] Sir William Pepperell was a descendant of the first of that name, who settled in Maine, and was knighted by William the Third. He was educated at Harvard University, and was afterwards one of the Council of Massachusetts. He was continued in that office under the mandamus of the King in 1774, and, of course, became very odious to the people. He was denounced by his neighbors, and in fear he fled to Boston. He and his wife started for England in 1775, but she died

on the passage. He was proscribed and banished by the act of 1778, and the following year his property was confiscated, under the conspiracy act. He was an active, benevolent and very useful citizen, and became one of the founders of the British and Foreign Bible Society. He was also President of the Association of Loyalists, in London, formed in 1779. He never returned to America. He died at his residence on Portman Square, in December, 1816, at the age of seventy years. He appears in West's celebrated picture, the "Reception of the American Loyalists by Great Britain, in 1783," a copy of which may be found in Lossing's *Field Book of the Revolution,* vol. ii. page 667.

[93] William Browne was a grandson of Governor Burnet, was owner of an immense landed estate, and was one of the hated Mandamus Councillors. He was an active and popular man in Massachusetts, prior to the Revolution. He was compelled to leave in 1776; and in 1779, his property was confiscated, and he became an exile in England. Afterward he was appointed Governor of the Bermudas. He died in England in 1802.

[94] John Erving, Jr., of Boston, was an addressor of both Hutchinson and Gage, and a Mandamus Councillor. He was therefore double-dyed in iniquity in the eyes of the Whigs. He fled to Halifax in 1776, and from thence to England. He was perpetually banished, and his property being confiscated by the conspiracy act of 1779,

he never returned to his native country. He died in England in 1816, at the age of eighty-nine years.

[95] Henry the Eighth, of England, established Protestantism as the religion of the State, at about the middle of the sixteenth century, and during the reign of his son Edward, which commenced in 1574, the tangible line of doctrinal difference between Luther and Calvin was drawn. The followers of the former allowed many of the ceremonials of the Church of Rome. Those of the latter were more austere, demanded more simplicity in the public worship, and great purity of life. On the latter account, they were called *Puritans*, in derision. They were afterwards persecuted by both the Roman Catholics and the English churchmen. Many fled to Holland, and from the *Puritan* congregation there, came the Pilgrim Fathers, who commenced settlements in New England, in 1620.

[96] Harrison Gray was Treasurer, or Receiver-General of Massachusetts. He was an addressor of Hutchinson, and one of Gage's Mandamus Council. He became greatly detested by the Whigs on that account, and especially because of a pamphlet which he wrote, in which he charged the Congress of Philadelphia with being drunk when they signed the *Continental Association*. A copy of the Association may be found in the journals of the first Congress, in 1774. At the evacuation

of Boston by the British, he went, with others, to
Halifax, and from thence to England, where he
died. On leaving, he parted with his only daughter, who was the first wife of Samuel Otis, father
of the late Harrison Gray Otis, of Boston. Mr.
Gray was an excellent man, in every relation of
life, and did not deserve the harsh language here
made use of by the poet.

[97] The Earl of Dartmouth succeeded the Earl
of Hillsborough as Secretary of State for the
Colonies in 1772, and was in that station when the
Revolution broke out. He was considered rather
friendly to the colonies at first; and was always
favorable to mild measures. He and Doctor
Franklin were warm personal friends.

[98] The "prime saint" alluded to was Governor
Hutchinson, who always professed great friendship
for the people of his native province. His own
letters proved his hypocrisy, for while he was
making these professions, he was writing to the
ministry, declaring the necessity, in order to
maintain government in Massachusetts, of destroying the charter, abridging what he termed *English
liberties*, making Judges dependant only upon the
Crown, and creating a nobility in America!
Some of these letters were secretly placed in the
hands of Dr. Franklin, then Provincial Agent at
the English Court, and he transmitted them to
Boston. Soon afterward, (1773,) finding himself
suspected of advising the ministry to employ op-

pressive measures, he declared, in a message to the Assembly, that he had ever been an advocate of the rights of the province contained in the charter, and the equal liberties of the colonists with other British subjects. His letters were then published, and gave the lie to all his pretensions. The excitement which they produced was intense, and, for a time, his person was in great danger.

[99] When Hutchinson fled to England, a spirit of revenge, uniting with his real sentiments respecting government in America, caused him to strongly urge Lord North to turn the screw of oppression still closer, and he remained a bitter and uncompromising enemy of the Americans.

[100] After the events at Lexington and Concord, Boston was menaced by an exasperated multitude, and General Gage became alarmed. He abandoned his haughty tone and demeanor, and sought an interview with the select men, as the municipal trustees were called. A town meeting was held on the 22d of April, and an agreement was entered into between the local authorities and the Governor, " That upon the inhabitants in general lodging their arms in Faneuil Hall, or any other convenient place, under the care of the select men, marked with the names of their respective owners, all such inhabitants that are inclined, might leave the town with their families and effects," &c., &c. The Tories remonstrated with Gage, and working

upon his fears in another way, caused him to put
obstacles in the way of the people who desired to
leave, and finally, to refuse to grant passes altogether. He concluded it was better to keep the
Whigs in the city, as hostages for the good behavior of their brethren outside, for really,

"They *were* the only guards that saved him."

[101] When the news of the skirmishes at Lexington and Concord swept over New England, the
people flocked toward Boston by hundreds and
thousands, resolved to chain the tiger upon that
peninsula, or drive him into the sea. Israel
Putnam, a veteran of the French and Indian War,
and then a brigadier-general of the Connecticut
militia, was among the earliest of the rallying
minute-men of the East, and took command of
the motley host by common consent, at first.
Gage well knew the spirit of the man, and was
in daily expectation that he would force his
way into Boston, and "mutton him;" in
other words, destroy him and his army. Putnam
was afterwards appointed one of the four major-generals, commissioned by Congress to assist in
the command of the Continental Army; and he
served his country well, until disabled by paralysis,
in 1779. He lived in retirement after the war,
and died in Brooklyn, Wyndham county, Connecticut, on the 29th of May, 1790, at the age of
seventy-two years.

[107] Numbers, chapter xxx.

[10] In 1766, the *Sons of Liberty*, in New York, as the associated patriots who opposed the Stamp Act were called, after dining at Montague's, and procuring the sanction of the Governor, erected a mast or tall pole a little north-east of the present City Hall, in front of Warren street, and upon it was inscribed, " To his most gracious majesty, George the Third, Wm. Pitt and Liberty." These poles were erected afterward, and elsewhere, and became known as " Liberty poles," a name which they still bear. Around these poles the patriots assembled, and near them they sometimes punished Tory offenders, by stripping them naked, pouring warm tar over them, and then emptying a bag of feathers upon them. There were certain large trees in Boston, Norwich, Charleston and other places, where the Whigs assembled, which were called *Liberty trees* These became very obnoxious to the friends of government, and attempts were often made to cut them down. The one in Boston, which stood at the corner of the present Washington and Essex streets, opposite the Boylston Market, was cut down by the British in 1775, with great parade. A soldier was killed by falling from its branches, during the operation, of whom some poetic wit of the day wrote:

> " Pale turned the wretch—he spread each helpless hand
> But spread in vain—with headlong force he fell,
> Nor stopped descending till he stopped in hell!"

[104] This is in allusion to the church discipline of New England, when a person was obliged to stand in the aisle, called the " broad alley," name the offence he had committed, and ask pardon of his brethren.

CANTO II

[1] This refers to the thrice-repeated words " Oh yes!" used in opening courts, and as a preface to verbal proclamations, and the commencement of the business of public meetings.

[2] The person here alluded to, was William Laud, Archbishop of Canterbury, who was the Primate, or Chief Ecclesiastical officer of England, during a portion of the reign of Charles the First. He succeeded Abbot as primate, in 1633, and at the same time he was the prime minister of State. He held these exalted offices with a firm and steady rein, and with great energy he endeavored to repress the Puritan spirit. The persecutions which he employed drove some of the best men from England to America; and, it is said, that even John Hampden, and Oliver Cromwell, were, at one time, on the eve of embarkation for the New World. Laud became very obnoxious to all who disliked the hierarchy, and he was accused of high **t**rimes, which were not proven against him. Popular

hatred demanded his blood. The peers, overborne by the prevailing sentiment, pronounced him guilty, and he was beheaded on Tower Hill, on the 10th of January, 1645, when 71 years of age. That was four years before his royal master met the same fate. Laud was an honest but mistaken man. We must judge him by the spirit of the times in which he lived.

[3] In the edition of M'Fingal, revised by the author and published in 1820, there are the four following lines, immediately preceding this:

> "Who'd seen, except for these restraints,
> Your Witches, Quakers, Whigs, and Saints,
> Or heard of Mather's famed *Magnalia*,
> If Charles and Laud had chanced to fail you?"

The allusion to Cotton Mather refers to his book called *Magnalia*, in which he gives a ridiculous history of pretended miracles which occurred during the first years of the settlement of New England. In his "Wonders of the Invisible World," Mather gave an account of the delusion known as the Salem Witchcraft. Mather was a man of learning, yet he was a believer in witches.

Although the settlements in America were nearly all made by private individuals, and at the expense of private capital, the King claimed to own the lands discovered by his subjects in the New World, and they were compelled to procure grants from him, by which certain privileges were given to the proprietor, who made the settlements. These charters were the original fundamental laws of all the colonies. That given to Rhode Island by Charles the Second remained in force as the Constitution of the State until 1843, when the people made a new one. The first charters were often annulled, and new ones were given; and those charters in which privileges were defined were regarded by the people with great reverence. I have already referred in Note 30, Canto I., to the boasts of English statesmen, concerning aids given to the colonists.

⁴ Although the ancient feud between France and England, as well as a difference in religion, caused the English and French settlers in America to regard each other as rivals, yet it was doubtless the quarrels of the parent government that made them actual and open enemies, and brought them into bloody conflicts. And in those wars the colonists bore much more than their own proper share of the burden.

⁵ Generals Braddock, Abercrombie, Amherst, Loudoun, Wolfe and others, were sent over to conduct the war that broke out in 1755, and oftentimes by their folly, arrogance, or tardiness, they thwarted the more enterprising provincials, and stood in the way of success. On the field where Braddock was killed, death and desolation were spread in all directions, until the fall of that officer, and others, placed the command in the hands of young Wash-

ington, when the fortunes of the day were immediately changed. In almost every instance, the provincial officers were more efficient than those of the regular army. The history of the tardiness and stupidity of Loudoun forms a disgraceful chapter in the records of England. Wolfe and Amherst were the most efficient of all the English officers who were sent to America during the French and Indian War.

⁶ The energy and justice of Pitt were greatly applauded by the Americans; and when, in the spring of 1759, his splendid scheme for the conquest of Canada was to be put into execution, the provincials flocked to the standards of their chiefs with such alacrity, that the quota of soldiers called for was far exceeded by numbers. When Amherst came, he found twenty thousand troops at his disposal, and many others were eager to join the royal army.

⁷ The first step toward the establishment of Episcopacy in America was at about the year 1748, when Dr. Secker, archbishop of Canterbury, not only proposed the matter, but offered the mitre to several Puritan divines. Whitefield, the celebrated field-preacher, said to Dr. Langdon, of Portsmouth, New Hampshire, at about that time, " I can't in conscience leave this town without acquainting you with a secret. My heart bleeds for America. O poor New England! There is a deep-laid plot against both your civil and religious

liberties, and they will be lost. Your golden days are at an end—you have nothing but trouble before you. . . . . . Your liberties will be lost.' He referred to the scheme then in preparation by the English hierarchy. The first important step was the sending over several Episcopal clergymen as missionaries, who had been ordained by the Bishop of London. These settled in the colonies; and those at the North, especially, became attached to the royal cause. The intention was to have the New England churches ruled by bishops; but the Revolution swept the whole plan into oblivion.

[b] The simple fact of sending troops to America to awe the people, produced much irritation in the provinces; but when the colonists were called upon to contribute toward the support of these troops, they regarded the matter as downright oppression. The New York Assembly refused to vote supplies, and for this contumacious act, Parliament, in 1767, passed an act, " prohibiting the Governor, Council, and Assembly of New York, passing any legislative act for any purpose whatever" This alarming disability caused the legislature of that province to make some concessions, yet the point was not yielded until 1769, when a small appropriation was made for the support of the troops. In Boston, the insolence of the troops greatly irritated the people, and finally they came to an open rupture early in March, 1770, which resulted in the death of several citizens. This

event is known in history as *The Boston Massacre.* So in Wilmington in North Carolina, and in Charleston in South Carolina, and other places, the people were exceedingly restiff under the frowns of a military despotism.

⁹ It has been asserted that a large portion of the old English peerage, created previous to the close of the reign of Charles the Second, have originated from the illegitimate progeny of the kings. It is to this fact, and the grievance of having such men hold all of the best offices of trust and emolument in the kingdom, that the author here alludes.

¹⁰ At that time the urgent calls of an exchequer, depleted by recent wars and increasing pensions, caused the levying of very heavy taxes, even in Scotland and Ireland, where, hitherto, they had been less than in England. The Scotch murmured, and the Irish endured the burden with a bad grace, while the English people themselves, borne down by taxation, sympathized with their brethren in America, in their resistance to the same form of oppression. The chief cause of complaint was the pensioning of, and giving sinecure places to, undeserving scions of royalty or the aristocracy. And the Americans justly complained that the best offices in the colonies were filled by such men, to the exclusion of native-born citizens, who could justly boast of superior intelligence and virtue.

¹¹ Sir David Dalrymple was a ministerial writer

of some eminence, and a lawyer and antiquarian of note in Edinburgh. He undertook at one time to prove that all of the celebrated British patriots, in the time of the civil war, were pensioners, in the pay of France. He based his charges upon the alleged fact, that the letters of the French ambassadors in England disclosed the significant secret, that thousands of guineas were paid by them to Algernon Sydney, John Hampden, &c. He also alleged that Admiral Russell defeated the French fleet at a time when he was under a solemn engagement, and had received a stipulated sum, to be beaten himself. How far truth will support a theory founded on these alleged facts, cannot be easily determined. But it was from premises like these, that Sir David argued that " public virtue was but a name."

[12] Dr. Samuel Johnson also wrote against the Americans. His pamphlet entitled *Taxation no Tyranny* is an able paper. He, too, had no faith in patriots so called, and in public virtue. Like Cardinal Richelieu, he believed that every man had his price. A poet of the time, in an epigram, intimated that the doctor's price was paid to him for his defence of ministers.

[13] This is in allusion to the noble words of Samuel Adams, in the first Continental Congress, when a proposition of Joseph Galloway to make concessions to Great Britain elicited a warm debate. Adams regarded the proposition as a concession to

tyranny, and, his soul kindling with patriotic zeal, he exclaimed: "I should advise persisting in our struggle for liberty, though it were revealed from Heaven that nine hundred and ninety-nine were to perish, and only one of a thousand were to survive and retain his liberty! One such freeman must possess more virtue, and enjoy more happiness, than a thousand slaves; and let him propogate his like, and transmit to them what he has so nobly preserved."

[14] Sir Jeffrey Amherst, who commanded the British troops in America, in the final conquest of Canada.

[15] Amherst declared, on the floor of the House of Commons, that with five thousand regular troops, he could march from one end of the continent to the other, unmolested. Gage repeated the foolish boast to Putnam, who instantly replied, "So you might, if they behaved themselves, and paid for what they got; if not, the women would knock your soldiers in the head with their ladles."

[16] Colonel Grant was a meritorious officer in the French and Indian War, and was the successful leader of an expedition against the Cherokees in 1761. He was a brigadier at the commencement of the Revolution, and led the division of the British army in the battle near Brooklyn, at the close of the summer of 1776, which first engaged the Americans under Lord Stirling. Grant made assertions simi-

lar to those of Amherst, and added that nothing would exceed the speed of the Americans in their flight before an enemy. On several occasions during the Revolution, General Grant was compelled to run swiftly *before* the "rebels" he affected so much to despise, but never *after* them. At this he seems to have been very expert, and

"Well skilled on runnings to decide."

[17] It is asserted that the roar of a lion will turn small beer sour. The lion is the emblem of Great Britain's courage and strength, and is the principal figure on the national escutcheon. It was originally a leopard, according to a record of the year 1252.

[18] Such declarations were continually made by North and his cabinet. They asserted the *right* of Parliament to tax the colonies, and declared the necessity of such a tax for the purposes of revenue.

[19] In the debate on the Boston Port Bill, in the spring of 1774, Mr. Van, a ministerial member of Parliament, used very violent language toward the people of Boston. "They ought to have their town knocked about their ears, and destroyed," he said, because of their destruction of the cargoes of tea in that harbor, a few months before; and concluded his tirade of abuse by quoting the words of Cato the Censor, concerning Carthage,

Delenda est Carthago—Carthage must be destroyed.

[20] It cannot be doubted that among the measures for crushing the rising rebellion in America, adopted by the British ministry early in 1774, was that of exciting the Indians on the frontiers of the white settlements against their neighbors. In this work, a little later, the sons of Sir William Johnson, in the Mohawk Valley, were engaged. Stuart, in the Carolinas, was busy among the Creeks and other frontier tribes; and the Governors of some of the provinces had, doubtless, secret instructions on this point. Governor Gage and Governor Dunmore, of Virginia, were known to be employed in this nefarious business in 1775. In the autumn of that year, Dr. Connolly, of Pittsburg, visited General Gage, at Boston, and soon afterward, while on his way toward the Ohio country, through Maryland, he was arrested as a suspicious character. Concealed in his saddle were papers, which revealed the fact that he was commissioned to arouse and lead the Indians against the people of Virginia. Governor Carleton, of Canada, was also engaged in the same business; and the effect of the agency of secret emissaries among the savages, was seen as the war progressed, in the terrible massacres everywhere committed by the Indians, under the protecting wing of British power. The horrid practice of employing the Indians was severely com-

mented upon in the British Parliament. A member attempted to justify the measure by saying, that they had a right to employ the means "which God and nature had put into their hands." The great Pitt scornfully repeated these words, and said, "These abominable principles, and this most abominable avowal of them, demands most decisive indignation. I call upon that right reverend bench (pointing to the Bishops), those holy ministers of the Gospel and pious pastors of the Church, I conjure them to join in the holy work, and to vindicate the religion of their God." But "those holy ministers" had no word of condemnation. In the Declaration of Independence the King was charged with endeavors "to bring on the inhabitants of our frontiers the merciless Indian savages," and the proofs of the truth of that charge were many and undeniable.

[21] Guy Carleton (afterward Lord Dorchester), was Governor of Canada from 1772 to 1781, when he succeeded Sir Henry Clinton as Commander-in-Chief of the British army in America. He was made Governor of Quebec, Nova Scotia, and New Brunswick in 1786. As a reward for long services he was raised to the peerage. He died in 1808, at the age of eighty-five years. It is due to his memory to say, that he doubtless was opposed to the employment of the savages against the Americans. He was a very humane man, as his kindness to American prisoners often proved.

Guy Johnson was a son of Sir William Johnson, by a sister of Brant, the great Mohawk Chief. He had great influence over the Iroquois, and in 1775 he, in connection with the Butlers and Brant, held a large council of Indians, composed chiefly of Cayugas and Senecas. After the war he was an Indian agent in Canada.

[22] Guy, Earl of Warwick, was called the Kingmaker. He was killed at the battle of Barnet in April, 1471. He is very celebrated in the martial annals of Great Britain.

[23] The Dun cow is celebrated in tradition as a fierce animal that roamed over a heath, and had killed many people. She was twelve feet in height from hoof to shoulder, and eighteen feet in length from the neck to the root of the tail. The young and fiery Guy undertook to kill the beast, in order to win a mistress. He did so, and the heath still bears the name of Dunsmore. This is supposed to be a myth, and that the cow was a Countess, who led a disreputable life, and ruined many young lords by winning their estates from them at card-playing. Guy beat her at the game, and so the destroyer was conquered.

[24] Among the threats of royal Governors in the slave-holding provinces, was that of giving these bond-servants their freedom, and letting them loose, like bloodhounds, upon their masters. And this was no idle threat. Nothing but the general attachment of the slaves to their masters prevented

the perpetration of the most frightful massacres.
When, in June, 1775, Lord Dunmore, the Governor
of Virginia, fled for safety to a British man-of-war,
his first vindictive and retaliatory efforts were to call
the slaves to his standard, under a promise of freedom. Many obeyed the call, and were in the battle at the Great Bridge, twelve miles from Norfolk, in December following. Hundreds of them
afterwards miserably perished. The same thing
was attempted, by authority, in the Carolinas; and
in Boston a company of negroes was formed and
regularly enrolled. Yet the negroes were not all
"loyal," for we find that, on one occasion, when
they had been ordered to assemble in Faneuil Hall,
to choose from among their number proper persons to clean the streets, Cæsar Merrian, in the
presence of Joshua Levering, moderator, dared to
oppose the measure, for which he " was committed
to prison, and confined until the streets were all
cleaned." The Declaration of Independence says,
" He has excited domestic insurrection among us,"
and these facts are the proofs.

[25] This was a specimen of M'Fingal's "second
sight," for there was, as yet, no Bishop in America

[26] The negroes who enlisted in the army in Boston were chiefly slaves of the whigs who had left
the town. They were dressed in the scarlet uniform of the British army, a color particularly
adapted to win the black man, who is fond of show

27 "The stones and all the elements with thee
  Shall ratify a strict confed'racy;
  Wild beasts their savage temper shall forget,
  And for a firm alliance with thee treat."
        Blackmore's Paraphrase of Job.

28 These were the materials employed against the Americans by the British ministry previous to the sending over German troops, mentioned in Note 15, Canto I.

29 When Gage proceeded to Boston to enforce the Bort Bill, he ordered two additional regiments to march there. They entered Boston with great display, and encamped on the Common, or Mall. Other troops soon joined them, and as the people refused to give them shelter, they all remained encamped on the Common during the summer of 1774. The contending political parties wrote and published much. *Massachusettensis* (See Note 75, Canto I.) began his essays, and John Adams soon answered them. Gage sent out proclamation after proclamation, and the patriots met him with "squib for squib" at every turn. His proclamations were very bombastic, and were much ridiculed. They were sometimes paraphrased in rhyme. The following is a specimen of one of these:

  "Tom Gage's proclamation,
    Or blustering denunciation,
    (Replete with defamation,)
  Threatening devastation

And speedy jugulation,
Of the New English nation,
Who shall his pious ways-shun."

This was the commencement. Then followed a paraphrase, and the whole ended with,

"Thus graciously the war I wage,
As witnesseth my hand,
TOM GAGE
By command of *Mother Carey*,
THOMAS FLUCKER, Secretary.

Flucker was the Secretary of Massachusetts under Gage. He was the father of Lucy, the wife of General Henry Knox, the Commander-in-Chief of the artillery of the Continental army.

[30] Gage's fears made him more of a tyrant than he wished to be. Alarmed by hostile demonstrations on all sides, he first stationed a strong guard upon Boston Neck, which connected the peninsula with the main, at Roxbury, with the avowed shallow pretence that he wished to prevent desertions from his ranks. He next commenced erecting a line of fortifications across the Neck. Boston carpenters could not be hired to do the work, and mechanics from New York were employed for the purpose. These things greatly irritated the people, because they were proofs of the manifest intention of Government to coerce them into submission to unjust laws.

[31] Matthew, xvii. 27.
[32] Numbers, Chapter xii.

[33] When Rome was invested by the Gauls, almost four hundred years before the birth of Christ, a noble band of citizens and soldiers shut themselves up in the Capitol. One night the Gauls climbed up the steep rocks of the Capitoline Hill, and were about to kill the sentinels and capture the garrison, when some geese, being awakened by the noise, cackled so loudly that they aroused the soldiers in time to save the Capitol, and perhaps the Roman Empire.

[34] See an account of Bishop Atterbury's trial, in the Histories of England. Francis Atterbury was Bishop of Rochester and Dean of Westminster. He favored the Stuarts, and being suspected of being in league with the old Pretender, son of James the Second, he was sent to the Tower on a charge of treason, in 1722. He was banished the following year, and died at Paris in 1732.

[35] Exodus, Chapter viii.

[36] A noodle meant simpleton. This term was much in use formerly.

[37] The exact origin of *Yankee Doodle*, our national air, is not positively known. There was a popular song adapted to the old air of Nancy Dawson, composed and sung in derision of Cromwell by the Cavaliers and other loyalists, which commenced thus:

> "Nankey Doodle came to town,
> Riding on a pony,
> With a feather in his hat
> Upon a macaroni."

A " doodle " is defined in the old English dictionaries, as " a sorry, trifling fellow," and the term was thus applied to Cromwell. A " macaroni " was a knot on the hat, on which a feather was fastened. In a satirical poem accompanying a caricature of William Pitt, published in 1766, in which he appears on stilts, the following stanza occurs:

"Stamp act! le diable! dat is de job, sir;
 Dat is in de stiltman's nob, sir,
 To be America's nabob, sir.
 Doodle, noodle, do."

The air of Yankee Doodle was known in New England, long before the Revolution, as " Lydia Fisher's Jig; " and in 1755, a surgeon in the British army at Albany, composed a song to that air, in derision of the uncouth appearance of the New England troops then assembled there. He called it " Yankee Doodle." The air was popular as martial music; and we find on record that when, in 1768, British troops arrived in ships in Boston harbor, " the Yankee Doodle tune was the capital piece in the band of music at Castle William." The change in spelling the first word from Yankey to Yankee, did not occur until after the Revolution. While the army under Washington was at Cambridge, in 1775, some loyal poet wrote a long string of doggerel verse, in derision of the New England people, and troops, commencing:

"Father and I went down to camp,
Along with Captain Goodwin,
There we *see* the men and boys
As thick as hasty-*puddin'*."

See Note 1, Canto I.

[38] The people in Boston, and the army there, after Gage's arrival, held toward each other the most bitter animosity, and that was often inflamed by the wicked or injudicious conduct of subordinate officers. Among sinners of this kind, was Lieutenant Colonel Nesbitt, who, at the beginning of 1775, took great pains to insult and injure the Americans. The country people sometimes came into town, to buy muskets for hunting. On one occasion Nesbitt instructed a soldier to sell one of them an old rusty musket. The purchaser was an inoffensive man, who sold vegetables, and paid the soldier three dollars for the gun. He was almost immediately seized under a false charge of carrying arms for a treasonable purpose, and thrown into the guard-house. Early the next morning punishment was adjudged, and he was stripped naked, furnished with a covering of tar and feathers, placed upon a cart, paraded the length of the city and back, and was taken to Liberty Tree. This *brave* act was performed by about thirty grenadiers of the 47th regiment, with fixed bayonets, and twenty drums and fifes playing the Rogue's March. The procession was headed by Nesbitt with a drawn sword. The indignant

people flocked to Liberty Tree, when the alarmed soldiers fled to their barracks, and the poor man was rescued.

The origin of the punishment by tar and feathers, has been fixed at the period of the Revolution, by most writers. According to the Pictorial History of England, vol. i. page 487, quoted in Duyckinck's Cyclopedia of American Literature, the "plumeopicean robe" is as old as the crusaders. Richard Cœur de Lion made the regulation that "A man convicted of theft or 'pickerie,' was to have his head shaved, and hot pitch poured upon his bare pate, and over the pitch the feathers of some pillow or cushion were to be shaken, as a mark whereby he might be known as a thief."

[39] Caligula was the most detested of the Roman Emperors, because of his ferocious and dissipated character. In the year of our Lord 16, he led an army to the shores of Gaul, for the purpose of invading Britain, but he did not embark. He there ordered a charge to be sounded, and a signal to be made for engaging an enemy. But no enemy of course, appeared. His soldiers were then directed to gather cockle-shells, to be sent to Rome as "spoils of the ocean," and these adorned the ridiculous triumph which a corrupt senate decreed for him.

[40] After a siege of ten years, ancient Troy was taken by the Greeks, through strategy. Finding they could not gain a forcible entrance into the

city, they constructed an enormous wooden horse, introduced many armed men into its body, and then made a pretended retreat toward the seashore, leaving the colossal beast near the walls. Sinon, one of the Greek warriors, went to Troy with his hands bound behind him, and solemnly assured the Trojans of the absolute abandonment of the siege by the Greeks. He then advised them to convey the great horse into the city, as a trophy. It was done, and during that night, Sinon opened the secret door in the side of the horse, and let out the armed Greeks. They surprised the Trojans, pillaged the city, and Troy fell!

[41] Colonel Leslie was one of the most useful of the British officers who came to America to " crush the rebellion." He arose to the rank of brigadier, whilst here, and was the last commander-in-chief of the British army at Charleston. His services at the south, under Cornwallis, were very highly commended, and he was generally esteemed by the Americans as a judicious, honorable, and humane commander.

[42] Marblehead was originally a part of Salem, and is about sixteen miles from Boston. It was remarkable for its fishermen at the time of the Revolution. Colonel Glover of the Continental Army, was from that town, and he employed many seamen from that place in conveying the Americans across the East river in the retreat of

the army from Brooklyn to New York in September, 1776. They also transported American stores in boats, from New York to Dobbs' Ferry.

[43] See Homer's description of the battle of the frogs and mice.

[44] On Sunday, the 26th of February, 1775, Colonel Leslie, with about three hundred men, was sent by Gage to seize some brass cannons and gun-carriages in possession of the Americans at Salem. They proceeded very secretly in a transport, which was moored at Marblehead before any of the soldiers appeared. They then rushed ashore, and commenced their march through the town. The people were engaged in public worship. Leslie's intentions being suspected, intelligence was immediately sent to Colonel Timothy Pickering, who called out the minute-men, and at an opened drawbridge near Salem, he confronted the British. A parley ensued, and Leslie agreed that if the people would close the bridge, and let him pass over in due form of invasion, he would immediately return. The terms of the treaty were complied with, and Leslie, like a sensible man, returned to Boston. Had he possessed the folly of some of the British officers, he would have given to Salem the honor which now belongs to Lexington, of having been the scene of the first bloodshed in the Revolution. As it was, the news went to England that in Salem "the Americans had hoisted the standard of liberty."

[45] Concord is a few miles from Lexington. There the stores were concealed, which Gage sought to capture or destroy, when he sent out the detachment that was checked by the minute-men at Lexington.

[46] General Gage, in his letter to Governor Trumbull concerning the affair at Lexington and Concord, pretended that his object in attempting to seize the stores and munitions of war at the latter place, was " to prevent civil war," by taking dangerous weapons out of the hands of the people!

[47] The important question after blood had flowed was, Which party began the war? A great many depositions were taken, and it was fully proven that the British troops first fired on the minute-men at Lexington, and killed several. The fire was promptly returned, however, in self-defence. In reference to this question, a writer in Anderson's *Constitutional Gazette*, published in New York in 1775, thus states the matter:

"*The Quarrel with America fairly stated.*

"Rudely forced to drink tea, Massachusetts in anger
Spills the tea on John Bull—John falls on to bang her;
Massachusetts, enraged, calls her neighbors to aid,
And give Master John a severe bastinade.
Now, good men of the law! pray, who is in fault,
The one who began, or resents the assault?"

[48] In former wars in America, the term *R gular* was applied to the British troops which came from

England, to distinguish them from the provincials, or new levies in America.

[49] This refers to the distance the British had to retreat after the affair at Lexington.

[50] In his account of the skirmishes, General Gage was pleased to say, "Too much praise cannot be given to Lord Percy for his remarkable activity throughout the whole day."

[51] This is explained in Note 3, Canto I.

[52] Gage endeavored to make light of the fact that he was so hemmed in by the Americans, who had gathered by thousands around Boston; and in his last proclamation, issued before the battle on Breed's Hill, he said, "With a preposterous parade of military arrangements, they affect to hold the army besieged."

[53] The Mystic river is on the northeast side of the Peninsula of Charlestown, on which are Bunker's and Breed's hills.

[54] In a late edition, the two following lines were added after the third line above this reference number:

"Nay, stern with rage, grins Putnam, boiling,
Plunder'd both Hogg and Noddle Island."

These were two islands in Boston Harbor, from which the Americans carried off all the cattle, sheep and swine, to prevent their falling into the hands of the British. Gage really had no alternative but to flee, or be driven
———"headlong to the sea."

Howe, who succeeded him in command, was reduced to the same alternative, and in March, 1776, he fled in his ships to Halifax, and the Americans, after a siege of several months, took possession of Boston. The British had been completely hemmed in upon the Boston peninsula from the 19th of April, 1775, until the 17th of March, 1776. Whenever they attempted to penetrate the country, or take possession of any of the islands in the harbor, they were met with determined resistance.

[55] Matthew viii., 32.

[56] The British man-of-war, *Cerberus*, arrived at Boston on the 25th of May, 1775, with Generals Howe, Clinton, and Burgoyne, three officers experienced in the military tactics of Europe, but unfit, in many respects, to conduct the war then just commenced. General William Howe was commissioned commander-in-chief, in place of General Gage, who was recalled and went to England soon afterward.

[57] Popular belief ascribed very evil effects to comets, and they were generally regarded as omens of calamity.

[58] Abijah White was a member of the Massachusetts House of Representatives, from Marshfield, and a warm adherent of the crown. He possessed very little judgment or discretion, and made himself very ridiculous by the way in which he manifested his zeal. When the loyalists of Marshfield, in public meeting, adopted resolutions which cen-

sured the people of Boston for destroying the tea, he was employed to carry them to that city, and lay them before the governor. Pretending a fear of being robbed of them by the way, he armed himself with gun, pistol and cutlass, and, mounting his horse, appeared like another Hudibras. On arriving at Boston, he caused the momentous document to be published. This act drew upon him some of the wrath, but more of the ridicule of the whigs, and he disappeared from public life forever.

⁵⁹ It is related as a fact, that some British officers, soon after Gage's arrival in Boston, while walking on Beacon hill one night, were much alarmed by noises in the air resembling the whizzing of bullets. They supposed they were missiles from noiseless air-guns, in the hands of the "rebels," and they fled precipitately to their quarters. They gave terrible accounts of this "nefarious business" in their letters to friends at home. The supposed bullets were the common *beetles*, with which we are all made familiar in the warm summer evenings.

⁶⁰ British officials, from ministers of state down to subalterns of lowest grade, were fond of threatening the Whigs with the pillory, whipping-post and gibbet. During the war, a son of Richard Henry Lee, of Virginia, was at school at St. Bees, in England. A gentleman one day asked the tutor, "What boy is this?" "A son of Richard Henry Lee, of America," he replied. The gentle-

man put his hand on the boy's head and remarked, "We shall yet see your father's head upon Tower Hill." The boy promptly replied, "You may have it when you can get it." That boy was the late Ludwell Lee, Esq., of Virginia.

[61] Called also "Heave-offering." Grain and fruit were waved or heaved toward the four cardinal points. It was a special present to the priests. See Numbers, chapter xviii.

[62] Cropping off portions of the ears, tying men to posts and whipping them, and confining them in a standing position in wooden frames called pillories, were barbarous modes of punishment, for light offences, at that time.

[63] Bunyan, in his *Pilgrim's Progress*, represents Christian as setting forth upon his journey with a very heavy bundle of all his sins, original and actual, upon his back.

[64] See Note 38, Canto II. The uniform alluded to was that of tar and feathers. The want of uniform dress in the American Army was a constant theme of ridicule with the British at the beginning of the war. Mr. Kidder, in his history of New Ipswich, gives, from the lips of an old soldier, a graphic description of his company when it joined the army of Gates a little while before the capture of Burgoyne. They all wore small clothes, and "not a pair of boots graced the company." Their coats and waistcoats were as various in colors "as the barks of oak, sumach, and other

trees of our hills and swamps could make them."
Their arms were as various as their costume; one
had a heavy "Queen Anne" musket, that had
' done service" in the conquest of Canada, and by
his side would be a boy, carrying a little Spanish
fuzee, captured, perhaps, at Havana. They all
used powder-horns instead of cartridge-boxes, and
occasionally a bayonet might be seen. A country
blacksmith made the swords of many of the officers, and in every particular they were as uncouth
as could well be imagined.

[65] The ships that " ravaged our coasts " were not
so benign as those of whom Waller sung:

> "Where'er our navy spreads her canvass wings,
> Honor to thee and peace to all she brings."

[66] Phœbus was another name for Apollo, or the
Sun.

[67] While the British occupied Boston, they sent
out military detachments to the neighboring islands
to seize sheep and cattle. Many skirmishes with the
Americans ensued on these occasions. And while
the army occupied New York, these expeditions
were very common, and sometimes resulted in considerable bloodshed. The Americans, also, had
frequent occasions to send out foraging parties during the war. It was one of these occasions in
which General Wayne was concerned, in New Jersey, opposite New York, that gave a theme to Major André when he wrote the famous poem called

"The Cow Chase." It was during a foraging expedition of the British from Charleston, up the Combahee river, in South Carolina, that the last battle of the Revolution was fought, in which Col. John Laurens was killed.

[68] Charlestown was burned during the battle on Breed's Hill, June 17th, 1775. Falmouth (now Portland, in Maine) was soon afterward destroyed by fire; and on the first of January, 1776, Norfolk, in Virginia, was also consumed, by order of Lord Dunmore. Later in the war, Danbury, Fairfield, and Norwalk were laid in ashes, and attempts were made to destroy other places. At Fairfield, the brutal Hessians, to whom Tryon gave full liberty to ravage and destroy, excited by strong drink, cruelly treated the women who fell into their hands, and whole families were driven into the swamps for shelter against their infernal lusts. Elsewhere, at the North and at the South, this kind of cruel warfare was frequently carried on by British hirelings, assisted by the Tories, who were justly more hated by the people than the Royal troops, or their German fellow mercenaries.

[69] Admiral Graves first appears in the drama of the Revolution, as Commander of the British fleet at Boston, in 1775. He last appeared in the contest in a sea-fight off the Capes of Virginia, a short time before the surrender of Cornwallis, in 1781, which was the concluding great military event of the war.

[70] Sir James Wallace, a fussy, blustering, naval commander, had charge of a little fleet of small vessels, in Narraganset Bay, to watch the movements of the Americans, plunder Rhode Island of sheep and cattle for the benefit of the British army in Boston, and to annoy the Americans generally. And he *did* annoy the people very much, and sometimes distressed them very much. When he first sailed into the harbor of Newport, he dispatched a letter, in the following words, to Captain Abraham Whipple, of Providence, who, in 1772, commanded an expedition which burned the *Gaspè* schooner, in Narraganset Bay:

"You, Abraham Whipple, on the 17th of June, 1772, burned His Majesty's vessel, the Gaspè, and I will hang you at the yard-arm.

JAMES WALLACE."

Whipple immediately replied:
" *To Sir James Wallace:*
SIR: Always catch a man before you hang him.
ABRAHAM WHIPPLE."

Wallace was driven out of Narraganset Bay in the spring of 1776, and in the autumn of 1777, he went up the Hudson river and assisted in burning Kingston.

[71] The Sandemanians were a small religious sect, so named because Robert Sandeman, a native of Perth, Scotland, was the founder. Their leading tenet of belief was that " Faith is a mere intellectual belief, a bare belief of the bare truth." They

also believed the Millennium near, and fixed upon the year 1793 as the time for its dawning. Sandeman came to America in 1764, and organized a church or society in Boston, and also in Danbury, Connecticut. He died and was buried at the latter place, in 1771, at the age of 53 years. His remains rest a few feet from those of General David Wooster.

[72] The unjust system of depriving whole families of property because of the political sins of the fathers, was commenced against the adherents of the Crown, first in Massachusetts in 1778, when a vast amount of property belonging to refugees who had fled, and some who ventured to remain, was confiscated. In 1779 the Massachusetts Legislature passed a conspiracy act, which sent into perpetual banishment a large portion of the same persons.

[73] The Tory party in New England worked upon the fears of the credulous and superstitious, by relating wonderful stories of strange appearances in the heavens, and strange noises in the air and under ground, and called them warnings of great troubles, if the Whigs persisted in their iniquitous proceedings. A remarkable meteor and Aurora Borealis were observed at the commencement of the war, and the superstitious were greatly alarmed.

[74] "The stars in their courses fought against Sisera."   *Song of Deborah*, Judges v. 29.

[75] A play upon the name of Lord North, the Prime Minister.

[76] Referring to a scheme proposed by Hutchinson and Oliver, in their letters to the British Ministry. See Note 98, Canto I. When the Carolinas were first settled, Shaftsbury and Locke proposed a magnificent scheme of aristocratic government in that portion of the New World, known as the Fundamental Constitutions. It contemplated orders of nobility, and all the paraphernalia of aristocracy except a King and Court. Even at that early day the *people* would not listen to such schemes, and they were abandoned.

[77] We have already noticed Hutchinson and Oliver. John Vassal, of Cambridge, was an Addresser of Hutchinson, in 1774, and the next year he was driven from his house by a mob, and made his abode in Boston. Without waiting for Confiscation Laws, the Committee of Safety appropriated some of his property to the public use. Such appropriation consisted chiefly of the products of the land, then in the fields. When Washington arrived at Cambridge, he made Mr. Vassal's house his head-quarters. It is now owned and occupied by Professor Longfellow, the eminent poet. Mr. Vassal went to England, with his family. His property was confiscated in 1778. At the age of sixty years, he died in England. The Vassals were among the earliest and most respectable of the settlers in New England.

[78] These were the titles of James, the brother of Charles the Second, who afterward became King of England. The province of New Netherland was given to him by his brother, and when, by actual conquest, he came into possession of it, the name of the city of New Amsterdam was changed to New York, and that of the town of Fort Orange, near the head of navigation on the Hudson river, to Albany.

[79] James Jauncy was at first inclined to be a whig, and was an associate with Jay and others on the Committee of Correspondence of Fifty. He was a member of the New York Assembly in 1775, and was one of the fourteen of that body who addressed General Gage on "the unhappy contest." He held the office of Master of the Rolls under the Crown; and his property was confiscated. After the war, he applied to the legislature of New York for a restoration of his property.

[80] Samuel Gales was also one of the fourteen Addressers of Gage, who were members of the New York Assembly in 1775.

[81] Colonel Christopher Billop was a man of property and influence. His house is yet (1857) standing on Staten Island, opposite Perth Amboy. It was there that Lord Howe held a conference with a committee of Congress on the subject of peace, in 1776. Colonel Billop was another member of the New York Assembly, who addressed

General Gage. He afterward commanded a corps
of Loyalists, was made a prisoner, and was confined in New Brunswick (New Jersey) jail, where
he was very harshly treated in retaliation of his
cruelties to two American prisoners in his custody.
After the war he went to the province of New
Brunswick, where he became a prominent man.
He died there in 1827, at the age of ninety years.

[62] See notice of Crean Brush, in Note 70, Canto I.

[63] See notice of Isaac Wilkins, D. D. Note 72,
Canto I.

[64] Frederick Phillipse, of the Phillipse Manor, in
Westchester County, New York, is here alluded
to. He was the brother of Mary Phillipse, whose
hand was once sought by George Washington,
when he was a provincial Colonel. Phillipse was
a member of the New York Assembly, and a colonel of militia; and finally, on account of his opposition to the whigs, he felt compelled to leave
his home and take refuge under British protection
in New York. From thence he went to England.
His large property was confiscated, and the British
Government afterwards allowed him, in compensation, about three hundred thousand dollars.
Colonel Phillipse died in England.

[65] This was Dr. Myles Cooper, already referred
to in Note 59, Canto I. He was a noted punster.

[66] John Vardell was educated at King's (now Columbia) College. He there prepared for the ministry, and became a professor in that institution for

a while. He went to England in 1774, to receive orders; and after the death of Dr. Ogilvie, he was appointed to the rectorship of Trinity Church, in New York. He did not accept it, being, as is supposed, in the employment of Government. Before he left for England, he had written several poetical satires on the Sons of Liberty, and was quite noted as a political writer in prose and verse.

[87] Two High Church clergymen of New York, already noticed.

[88] In note 9, Canto II, we have referred to the materials of which the old peerage of England was created. Adam was " created " of the dust of the ground. So the English technical phrase of " creating " a peer seems to be very appropriate, when we turn back to that old peerage, for surely it was of " low degree."

[89] See Note 47, Canto II, concerning the responsibility of striking the first blow.

[90] These are the Alleghany Mountai s, which extend from the State of New York to that of Georgia. They were then on the western frontier of the English settlements in America.

[91] The province of Georgia had not joined the union when the first Canto (of which this is a part) of McFingal was written. Georgia was represented in the next Congress, however.

[92] See Note 29, Canto II.

[93] Demosthenes pursued a course of very severe

self-training, so as to excel in oratory. In order to acquire for his voice a mastery over greater sounds, he used to stand upon the sea-shore, in storms, and declaim amidst the roar of the waves. By this means he was enabled to make his words heard and heeded in the tumult of a great assembly.

[94] See Note 25, Canto I.

[95] At that time, and until a quite recent period, the pulpits in this country were covered by a canopy called a "sounding board," to assist in making the preacher's voice heard by the whole congregation. Drawings of such pulpits may be seen in Lossing's *Pictorial Field-Book of the Revolution*, vol. i. p. 254, and vol. ii. p. 215.

[96] The Parcæ or Fates of ancient mythology were *Clotho* the spinster, who spins the thread of our existence; *Lachesis*, the allotter of our destinies; and *Atropos*, the unchangeable, whose shears clip the thread when life's mission is fulfilled.

[97] The Furiæ of mythology were *Alecto*, the unceasing; *Megæra*, the envier or denier; and *Tisiphone*, the blood-avenger.

[98] See Æsop's Fables.

[99] Genesis, Chapter xi.

[100] On some day in the week previous to the administration of the sacrament of the Lord's Supper in the New England Churches, a sermon was preached which was called a lecture, and that

day was known as lecture-day. These lectures were generally very thinly attended; a fact here alluded to by the poet.

CANTO III.

[1] See Note 103, Canto I.

[2] See *Gulliver's Travels*, by Dean Swift. The Brobdignagians are represented as a race of giants.

[3] "His spear, to equal which the tallest pine
  Hewn on Norwegian hills, to be the mast
  Of some great Admiral, were but a wand."
      Milton's *Paradise Lost*, Book I.

[4] At an early period of the contest, after the close of the session of the first Continental Congress in the autumn of 1774, the Americans used a flag with thirteen stripes, alternate red and white, to signify *union*. The stars on a blue ground were not used until late in 1777. Congress adopted the following resolution on the 14th of June of that year: "That the flag of the thirteen United States be thirteen stripes, alternate red and white; that the Union be thirteen stars, white, in a blue field, representing a new constellation." This Canto was written at the close of the contest.

[5] A mixed liquor, consisting of beer and spirits sweetened, and warmed by thrusting a hot iron into it.

[6] A female, celebrated by the ancient poets as skilled in magic arts and a knowledge of subtle poisons. She inhabited an Island, and all those who approached her were first feasted, and then, on tasting the contents of her magic cup, were changed into swine. She may properly be regarded as the representation of Alcohol, or of sensual indulgence in general.

[7] Nectar, in mythology and poetry, was the beverage used by the Gods.

[8] At that time fire engines were not introduced into this country. Leather buckets were kept in almost every house, and especially by the members of fire companies, to be used for the purpose of extinguishing fires. One set of men were appointed to use instruments for breaking into or pulling down buildings, and others, called " bucket men," supplied water.

[9] From time immemorial high poles, called *May-poles*, have been raised in England on the first day of May, and profusely garlanded with leaves and flowers in honor of the day, the ushering in of the summer wealth of the land. May-poles were places for joyful gatherings of the young, and doubtless suggested liberty-poles as the rallying points for public meetings. See Note 103, Canto I.

[10] Genesis, Chapter xi.

[11] Alluding to the electric conductors, or lightning rods, of Dr. Franklin, then becoming quite common in America and Europe.

[12] See Note 7, Canto I.

[13] Numbers, Chapter xxi. v. 9.

[14] The great Charter of England, obtained by the English Barons, of King John, at Runnymede, in the year 1215. In other words, a *fundamental constitution*, which guaranties rights and privileges.

[15] This is in allusion to the depreciation of the Continental paper money. Congress ascertained the cause of its declension at different periods, by what was called a Scale of Depreciation.

[16] A grand national festival of the Jews, held every fiftieth year, when all debts were cancelled, all prisoners and slaves were liberated, and when all lands and estates, whether they had been sold or mortgaged, were restored to the original proprietor. It was ushered in with trumpets and the most vehement demonstrations of joy.

[17] The courts of justice were everywhere closed at the commencement of the war, and those Judges who had been appointed by the Crown, and persisted in holding their seats, were driven from the court-rooms by the people, who assembled in multitudes, armed with white staves, the insignia of order.

[18] Alluding to the seizure of the property of Tories or Loyalists in the neighborhood of Bos-

ton, after their flight into that city. See Note 163, Canto IV.

[19] An old method of mild punishment, used even as far back as the time of the early Jews. The feet were confined in a wooden frame-work, so that the sitting delinquent could not move them, and in that situation he was subjected to the scoffs and rude insults of passers by. Hudibras, the great prototype of M'Fingal, was subjected to such punishment.

[20] The Loyalists often taunted the Whigs because some of their leaders were mechanics and tradesmen. In the temporary theatres established by the British in Boston, New York, and Philadelphia, during the war, these taunts formed a staple of the amusements. And these were continued long afterward. On one occasion a play was in course of performance in a London theatre, in which American officers were represented as mechanics of every kind. In the midst of the hilarity which the play occasioned on that account, an American sailor in the gallery shouted, "Hurrah! England whipt by cobblers and tailors!" The tables were turned upon John Bull.

[21] Unfortunately for Benedict Arnold, when his overt act of treason became known, he had not the redeeming antecedents of a good character to fall back upon. In early life he was an apothecary, and those with whom he served an apprenticeship in Norwich, Connecticut, set him up in

business in New Haven, where he also kept books and a general store. His sign—"B. Arnold, Druggist, Bookseller, &c., from London,"—is yet in existence. He also became interested in the West India trade, and made several voyages thither. He sometimes traded in horses; and it is said that the minute knowledge of the city of Quebec, displayed by him when he led troops across the wilderness to that place, in 1775, was obtained during his previous visits there for the purpose of buying horses. He finally failed in business, became a bankrupt, and was charged with saving a good deal of money by perjury. In this sentence there is an allusion to a curious lawsuit which he instituted against a brother skipper for slander.

[22] The author here remarks, in a Note, that "M'Fingal having here inserted the names and characters of several great men, whom the public have not yet fully detected, it is thought proper to omit sundry paragraphs of his speech in the present edition." These were never added.

[23] *Hudibras*, a satirical epic by Samuel Butler, is one of the few productions of that kind aimed at living characters or systems, which have survived their age. *Hudibras* is a cavalier burlesque of the extravagant ideas and rigid manners of the English Puritans of the Civil War and the Commonwealth. It was published after the restoration of monarchy; and it is understood that *Sir Hudibras*, the chief hero of the epic, was the

representation of Sir Samuel Luke, a well known Bedfordshire gentleman, one of Cromwell's favorite officers. His character is strongly marked by the peculiarities of that period. Butler's model for the actions of his hero was Don Quixotte, of Cervantes. Hudibras is considered not only the best burlesque of the Puritans, but the best satire in the English language.

[24] This is a thrust at the many glaring defects in the *Articles of Confederation*—the original constitution of the Federal Union. They served a good purpose while the union was cemented by the necessities of the existing war; but when Congress attempted to control the action of any of the States, it was powerless. These defects were so grave, that Washington and others took measures to have a revision of those fundamental statutes. A convention for that purpose was called, when it was found to be wiser to make a new machine than to attempt to patch up the old one; and a second convention framed the present Federal Constitution, in the year 1787.

[25] In issuing bills of credit, and in other transactions, Congress " pledged the faith of the United States," when, in fact, the States were not individually bound, by the old confederation, to redeem that pledge. The British ministry would not recognize the Congress as a legal body, and for a long time refused to hold any communication with its members, except as private individuals. And

General Howe, under ministerial instructions, at first addressed letters to the American commander-in-chief, as "Mr. Washington," alleging that his commission was not valid, because not given by a legal body. Of course the general refused to receive any communications thus addressed, and Howe was compelled to yield.

[26] Roger Bacon was a wonderful philosopher of the thirteenth century. He became a Franciscan monk, but his scientific discoveries and pursuits were so far above the comprehension of his associates and the age in which he lived, that he was generally regarded as a magician. Many stories of his magic arts were circulated; among others, that he possessed a human head of brass, out of which issued wise oracles. His fellow-monks became afraid of him, discarded his books, and finally procured his imprisonment for twelve long years. He undoubtedly discovered gunpowder and the telescope, and made many wonderful experiments in chemistry. In his treatises he couched his information in allegorical figures, and the then ignorant world was left to guess at his meaning. All may be interpreted by the light of science at the present time.

[27] This political plan of Trinculo, the jester, in the *Tempest*, may be found in the old folio editions of Shakspeare, but, for some reason, it has been expunged by his commentators, and does not now appear.

[28] The Centipede.

[29] The English Constitution comprehends the whole body of laws by which the British people are governed. Lord Bolingbroke made this nice distinction : " This assemblage of laws is distinguished from the term *government* in this respect ; that the *Constitution* is the rule by which the sovereign ought to rule at all times, and *government* is that by which he does govern at any particular time."

[30] See Note 76, Canto I.

[31] We have already alluded in Note 83, Canto I., to the destruction of tea in Boston harbor. It was done immediately after the breaking up of a popular meeting in the Old South Church, Boston, on the evening of the 16th of December, 1773. Mr. Josiah Quincy had pronounced an eloquent and stirring speech in the course of the afternoon. Twilight approached, and a call was made for candles. At that moment, a person in the gallery, disguised as a Mohawk Indian, raised the warwhoop, and was immediately answered from without. Another voice cried out, " Boston Harbor a tea-pot to-night ! Hurrah for Griffin's wharf ! " At that wharf the two tea-ships were moored. The meeting broke up in great excitement, and several persons, disguised as Indians, were seen to cross Fort Hill to Griffin's wharf. There was evident concert of action, and about fifteen or twenty persons thus disguised, with others differently con-

cealed, went on board the ships, deliberately took the chests of tea from the holds, broke them open, and cast their contents into the water. Three hundred and forty-two chests of tea were thus destroyed.

[32] The tea-ships were watched for twenty successive nights by parties of young men, to prevent the landing of the cargo. Under the Indian disguise, when the tea was destroyed, might have been seen ruffled shirts and laced vests; for those who performed that act were among the most respectable residents of Boston. Samuel Adams, the sturdy patriot, was one of them.

[33] The *moccasin* is the flexible Indian shoe, generally made of the tanned deer-skin, and is often highly ornamented.

[34] Wampum was the *money* of the Indians, and constituted expensive ornaments. It was made of the clear parts of the clam-shell, wrought into the form of small cylinders, like the beads of our day known as *bugles*, and about half an inch in length. They were arranged in *strings* and *belts*. When used for ornaments, they were disposed in alternate layers of white and black. As a circulating medium, they were valued at about two cents for three black beads, or six of the white ones. They were strung in parcels to represent a penny, three pence, a shilling, and five shillings of white, and double that amount in black. The allusion to " laces " refers to the respectable charac-

ter of the persons engaged in the destruction of the tea, as mentioned in a preceding note.

[35] That is, *painted* their faces. A single coat of paint is technically called a priming.

[36] The British soldiers, whose coats were made of scarlet cloth, were called Red-coats. In allusion to the same color, the provincial troops in the French and Indian war sometimes called the British Regulars, "lobsters."

[37] Governor Hutchinson was very much alarmed at the proceedings of the populace in destroying the tea, and very early the next morning he retired secretly to his country-seat at Milton, a short distance from the city. There he received an intimation that the mob was coming to pull down his house. With the utmost haste he escaped across the fields. The story was current at the time, that he was half-shaved by the barber when the alarming news reached him, and that in such plight—"in the suds" and bare-headed, he fled.

[38] See Note 85, Canto I.

[39] This alludes to the general breaking-up of all the councils of the royal governors in the colonies. These officials, unable to stem the current of public opinion and popular indignation, were compelled to relinquish their power and leave the country.

[40] Although some of the earlier organizations of the Sons of Liberty took place in the city of New York, yet the Loyalists held sway there in the public councils longer than in any other province.

When the Provincial Congress met on the 22d of May, 1775, its political complexion greatly disappointed the people; for much timidity prevailed in the Assembly, and under the influence of Governor Tryon and the municipal authority, a majority of the members were favorable to conciliatory measures, instead of vigorous preparations for defence. For this reason New York was taunted as loyal, when the great mass of the people were really whig to the core.

[41] When the skirmishes at Lexington and Concord became known in New York, Captain Isaac Sears, one of the boldest of the patriots of the day, was in custody on a charge of making treasonable propositions to the people. He was about to be taken to prison, when the populace took him forcibly from the officers, and bore him in triumph through the town, preceded by a band of music and a banner. This is the occurrence alluded to by Dr. Auchmuty in Note 57, Canto I. The people also took possession of the City Hall, armed themselves, and, led by John Lamb, Marinus Willett, John Morin Scott, and others, they embargoed all vessels in the harbor, laden with provisions for the British army in Boston. A cargo of rum for the patriots arrived. The collector of the port would not allow it to be landed. Sears and Lamb, with a large concourse of people, took possession of it, carried it to its destination in the city, and, returning to the custom-house, they demanded and

d the keys of that establishment, dismissed the employées, and closed the building. All the money and arms in the custom-house were seized; and during the summer many of such overt acts of rebellion were committed by the highly exasperated people. Tories were insulted; and on one occasion, when the Sons of Liberty were carrying off the cannon from Fort George and the Battery, and the *Asia* man-of-war fired upon them, the story was circulated that the city was about to be pillaged and burnt. Hundreds of men, women and children, frightened by the rumor, hurried off at midnight beyond the suburbs of the doomed town.

[42] This is in allusion to the quandary in which events placed William Smith, an eminent lawyer of New York, who seemed very desirous of being on the strongest side. He first opposed the measures of Great Britain, but finally adhered to the crown, and became a very decided Loyalist. He was brother to Joshua Hett Smith, who figured in the Arnold and André episode. Smith afterward became Chief Justice of Canada.

[43] Burning or hanging the effigy of an obnoxious officer was a common practice, and is still continued. It was an indication of the public sentiment against a man, and was practised here in imitation of a former custom of the English, in burning annually effigies of the Pope, the Devil, and the Pretender.

⁴⁴ In almost every case of effigy burning, that of the Devil was associated with the mortal offender. Thus, when in 1765 a mob in New York burned the effigy of Lieutenant-Governor Cadwallader Colden, they placed an image of the Devil, with a *boot* in his hand, by his side. The boot (used also in caricatures of that period) was a representation of the Earl of Bute, mentioned in Note 7, Canto I., because of a similarity in the orthoepy.

⁴⁵ William Tryon had figured as an oppressor, from 1768 to 1771, in North Carolina, where a party calling themselves *Regulators*, in the western part of the State, raised the standard of rebellion. He became governor of New-York, and held that office when the war broke out. Like other royal governors, he was compelled to yield to popular indignation, and he retaliated as a military leader. We shall meet him again.

⁴⁶ Joseph Galloway was an influential and very popular Whig leader in Pennsylvania at the commencement of troubles. He had worked shoulder to shoulder with Dr. Franklin in the Pennsylvania Assembly against the Proprietaries, and was a member of the First Continental Congress in 1774. After a while, when there appeared no chance for reconciliation with Great Britain, he wavered; and in 1776 he abandoned the Whigs, wrote much against them, and became one of the most violent and proscriptive Loyalists of the time. He joined the royal army in New York, and from thence he

went to England in 1778, where he remained until his death in 1803. Just before his escape, a trunk was put on board a vessel in the Delaware, directed to Joseph Galloway, Esq. It contained only, as Shakspeare says,

"A halter gratis, and leave to hang himself."

His examination before the House of Commons was a remarkable episode in the history of that period. He was in continual correspondence with Loyalists in America for many years, upon subjects connected with the war. His estate in Pennsylvania, valued at $200,000, was confiscated; but a greater portion of it was afterward restored to his daughter, it having been originally derived from his wife.

[47] Mainprize, in law, is a writ directed to a sheriff, commanding him to take sureties for the prisoner's appearance, and to let him go at large. The allusions in this sentence are to the retreat of the British, after the skirmishes at Lexington and Concord. The minute-men, concealed behind stone-walls, bushes and buildings, galled them terribly. A greater part of the loss of the enemy on that day occurred from this mode of warfare.

[48] It was a favorite method of the royal officers, when speaking of the "rebels," or in making propositions to them, to say, "The door of mercy is shut," or "it will soon be shut," and "Vengeance shall sleep no more."

[49] Dagon, the chief idol-god of the Philistines, represented with the body of a man, and the tail of a fish. 1 Samuel v. 1–5.

[50] The Tory clergy always spoke of the king as The Lord's Anointed.

[51] Joshua, chapter vi.

[52] When the people had fairly lifted the arm of open resistance, they would not acknowledge the king as ruler in any form. Henry Laurens boldly asserted his independence in this particular, even while a state prisoner, on a charge of treason, in the Tower of London, in 1781. He was at first treated very rigorously, but the people of England became so clamorous because of the injustice, that ministers were very anxious to relieve themselves of the odium. He was offered pardon if he would ask it. He nobly refused, because he had done nothing that required pardon. Then the ministry procured bail for him, intending that his release from confinement, under that form of law, should be perpetual. When, in reading the form, the clerk of the court repeated the words, " Our sovereign Lord and King," the prisoner immediately said, " Not *my* Sovereign," and refused to acknowledge George the Third as such. He was bailed, and then joined the commission to negotiate for peace between the two countries.

[53] Ovid's Metamorphoses, Book 12. The Lapithæ and Centaurs were hostile tribes of Thessaly.

The latter, because always seen on horseback, were said to be half men and half horses.

⁵⁴ Bacchus was the god of Wine—the tutelar deity of inebriates—a personification of sensual indulgence.

⁵⁵ Pallas was one of the names of the goddess Minerva, as opposed to the wild war-god, Mars; and she was the patroness and teacher of just and scientific warfare. She was the presiding deity in the Parthenon at Athens.

⁵⁶ Mars was the great god of War in the Greek mythology.

⁵⁷ Iris was the daughter of *Thaumas and Electra*—Wonder and Brightness—and was the goddess of the Rainbow.

⁵⁸ In this the reader will readily observe the allusions to the single combats of Paris and Menelaus, as described by Homer; and of Æneas and Turnus, mentioned by Virgil. Also of Michael and Satan, in Milton's Paradise Lost, Book VI.

⁵⁹ It was the fashion in New England at that time for Judges to wear swords, on the bench.

⁶⁰ Vulcan was the god of Fire, the great mechanic of the Greek mythology. Mount Etna and other volcanoes were regarded as his forges, and, according to the legends, he made implements of war for the old Grecian heroes.

⁶¹ ——— "The sword
Was given him tempered so that neither keen
Nor solid might resist its edge: it met

> The sword of Satan with *steep force* to smite
> Descending, and in half cut sheer."
>
> Milton's *Paradise Lost*, Book VI.

[62] Milton's *Paradise Lost*, Book II.

[63] This idea is from Juvenal, Satire 15.

[64] Alluding to the large people described in *Gulliver's Travels*, already mentioned, and to the popular belief that the Patagonians who inhabit the southern extremity of South America, were giants in stature.

[65] "And earth self-balanced on her centre hung."
  Milton.

[66] Aristophanes, in his Comedy of The Clouds, represents Socrates as hoisted in a basket. The object was to aid him in contemplation.

[67] The hatchel was an implement used in domestic manufacture to clean the coarser from the finer fabric of the flax, when preparing it for spinning. It was made of a piece of plank, with a large number of iron spikes driven through, and standing upright and close together. Through them the flax was drawn by hand, and the *tow* was separated from the finer fibre.

[68] See Note 19, Canto III.

[69] At that time the barbarous practice of clipping off a part or the whole of the ears of criminals was in vogue. It was called *cropping*.

[70] See Note 87, Canto I.

[71] Israel Williams was a member of the Massachusetts Assembly for many years, and became a

Mandamus Councillor in 1774. That fact brought Whig vengeance upon him. Though old and quite infirm, a mob took him from his house one night, carried him several miles, and put him into a room with fire. They then closed the doors and the top of the chimney, and kept him there in the smoke several hours. On being released he was compelled to sign a sort of recantation, drawn up by one of his tormentors.

[72] Thomas Oliver, of Cambridge, who mingled but little in politics. He was the last Royal Lieutenant-Governor of Massachusetts. His house was mobbed on the morning of September 2, 1774, because of his refusal to resign his seat as President of the Mandamus Council. They compelled him to make a sort of resignation in writing. Governor Oliver went to Halifax with the British troops, and from thence to England. He died at Bristol in 1815.

[73] See Note 59, Canto I.

[74] It is a curious fact, that the mobs in New England at that time always conducted their proceedings after the prescribed legal forms, when they tried and condemned Tories.

[75] This was in retaliation and imitation of the outrageous conduct of Colonel Nesbitt, mentioned in Note 38, Canto II. Sometimes those who received a coat of tar and feathers were placed astride a rail, and were thus paraded through the town.

[76] The Jewish kings were "anointed" by the High Priest before they were crowned, by having perfumed oil poured upon their heads. Hence the cant of Tory clergymen at that time, in calling King George "The Lord's Anointed." To this day an allusion to the ancient practice is contained in the expression " By the Grace of God, King," &c.

[77] See Claudian's *Gigantomachia*.

[78] Enceladus was one of the Giants or Titans who warred against Jove. As he fled, Minerva flung the Island of Sicily upon him, when, according to the poets, his motions caused the eruptions of Ætna.

[79] Maì was the mother of Mercury. See Note 24, Canto I.

[80] "A seraph winged; six wings he wore, to shade
His lineaments divine."
Milton's *Paradise Lost*, Book V.

[81] The Gorgons were three sisters—*Stheno, Euryale, and Medusa*, whose hairs were entwined with serpents, and they had wings of gold. Their hands were of brass, and their bodies were covered with impenetrable scales. Their teeth were as long as the tusks of a wild boar, and they turned to stone all those upon whom they fixed their eyes. *Chimera* was a terrible monster, that vomited fire. It had the head and neck of a lion, the body of a goat, and the tail of a serpent.

[82] Plato's famous definition of man was, *animal*

bipes implumis: "a two-legged animal without feathers."

[83] In ancient Rome, the union of two men in the same office was called a Duumvirate. Several kinds of offices were thus filled by two persons at the same time.

[84] Livy mentions the fact that an owl having been discovered in Rome, it was considered an omen of great evil. It was caught, taken from temple to temple, where lustrations were performed, and in great and solemn procession the Romans conducted the ill-omened bird beyond the walls, and set it at liberty in the forest.

[85] Votes were frequently passed at town meetings in New England, with a view to prevent the augmentation of prices of various articles, and to stop the depreciation of Continental money.

[86] A shell-fish which often adheres to the bottoms of ships at sea (as well as rocks and timber) in such quantities as to impede their progress.

[87]
"I hear a voice you cannot hear,
 That says I must not stay."
                    Ticknell's *Ballad*.

[88] In the debate on Lord North's first proposition in Parliament, in February, 1775, to use coercive measures against the Colonies, the celebrated John Wilkes, then a member of the House of Commons, took a conspicuous part in favor of the

Americans. He declared that " a proper resistance to wrong was *revolution,* not *rebellion,*" and prophetically intimated that if the Americans were successful in the struggle then commenced, they might, in after times, celebrate the Revolution of 1775, as the English did that of 1688, when they drove the last of the Stuart kings from the throne.

CANTO IV.

[1] The Tories during the Revolution, being not only in the minority, but more hated by the Whigs than were the British soldiery, were compelled to use great caution, and their secret meetings were held in cellars and other lurking-places.

[2] The great hall or council-chamber of evil spirits. A description of it, in *Paradise Lost,* Book I., is one of the most sublime creations of Milton's genius, and has been embodied by art, by the fine pencil of Martin of our day.

[3] In all New England cellars, *bins* are furnished for vegetables in winter. They are general y about four feet in height, and form good plac s for concealment.

[4] —" His form had not yet lost
All its original brightness, nor appeared
Less than Archangel ruined."
              Milton's *Paradise Lost,* Book ᐧ

⁵ It must be remembered how the Whigs had just robed poor Squire McFingal in tar and feathers.

⁶ See Note 6, Canto I.

⁷ See Note 98, Canto I.

⁸ Drunk on flip. See Note 5, Canto III.

⁹ Tar is procured from the pine and fir trees, by burning the wood by a close smothering heat.

¹⁰ "To drive the deere with hound and horne,
Erle Percy took his way;
The child may rue that is unborne,
The hunting of that day."

Chevy Chase.

¹¹ John Malcolm was a Scotchman, who settled in North Carolina after the famous rebellion of 1745. He was aid to Governor Tryon in 1771, when he went against the Regulators. [See Note 12, Canto IV.] He afterward became a custom-house officer at Falmouth (now Portland), in Maine; and early in 1774, he was in a similar position in Boston. He was an insolent man. One day he struck a tradesman for an alleged insult, and a warrant was issued for his arrest. The constable pretended he could not find him. A mob gathered about his house, when he thrust a sword through a broken window and wounded one of them. They broke in, found him in a chamber, lowered him by a rope from a window to a cart, tore off his clothes, tarred and feathered

him, and dragged him through several of the streets, with a rope around his neck, to Liberty Tree. From there he was taken to a gallows on Boston Neck, beaten, and threatened with death. In the course of an hour, he was conveyed to the extreme north end of the town; and then, after being bruised, and benumbed with cold for four hours, they took him back to his house. What became of him afterward, is not on record. He was despised by both parties, and became equally malevolent toward Whigs and Tories.

[12] The rapacity of officials in North Carolina, caused a great increase in the taxes of the province during the adminstration of Governor Tryon. The oppression was real—not an abstract *principle*, as in New England. The people in the interior associated for protection, and as already mentioned, they called themselves *Regulators* of public affairs. In the spring of 1771, their operations became open rebellion, and Tryon marched to subdue them with a strong militia force. The belligerents met on the Allamance, a tributary of the Haw, in Allamance County. While in opposing battle order, Malcolm, Tryon's aid above mentioned, was sent with a flag of truce. Recent perfidy on the part of Tryon, made the Regulators reckless of the rules of war, and they immediately fired on the bearer. Malcolm took to his heels, and, as tradition avers, the buttons of his small

clothes gave way in his haste. "He saved his life," however, and cared little for the ridicule.

[13] There is in the scene that follows, a general allusion to the appearance and speech of Hector's Ghost, in the second book of Virgil's Æneid.

[14] In 1715, a son of James the Second of England, who had been acknowledged king of that realm, as James the Third, by Louis the Fourteenth of France, set up his standard in Scotland, and caused a rebellion there. It was suppressed, and the *Pretender*, as the prince was called, escaped to the continent. In 1745, his son, Charles Edward, landed in Scotland, proclaimed his father king of Great Britain, and caused another serious rebellion. That, too, was suppressed the following year, and many of the Highlanders who were implicated came to America, and settled in the Carolinas, as voluntary or involuntary refugees. Among them was the famed Flora McDonald. This was "the last rebellion" alluded to by the poet.

[15] "Leaving the old, both worlds at once they view,
Who stand upon the threshold of the new."
Waller.

[16] Æneas was a celebrated Trojan warrior, whose adventures and wanderings form the subject of Virgil's Æneid.

[17] Orpheus was a Greek poet, musician, and philosopher. His beloved wife Eurydice died, and

the disconsolate husband determined to descend to the regions of Pluto, and attempt to induce the powers of the lower world to allow her to return to the domain of light. His music charmed all the gods of the infernal regions. His wife was released, and allowed to follow him, on condition than he should not look back upon her until they had passed the confines of darkness. His impatience made him violate the conditions, and she was lost to him for ever.

[18] Erebus, in the old mythology, or Orcus, in the ancient Latin religion, was the region of darkness. They were the same as Hades and Pluto of the Greeks.

[19] Milton's *Paradise Lost*, Book xi.

[20] Milton's *Paradise Lost*, Book xi. Euphrasy is a genus of plant, sometimes called eye-bright. Rue is a bitter plant, and the two compounded, were formerly used in making eye-water to strengthen the vision.

[21] The general rising of all the colonies to resistance, after the meeting of the first Continental Congress in the autumn of 1774, is here alluded to. Each colony had its particular flag.

[22] The American Congress resolved, in the summer of 1775, to invade Canada. An army under General Schuyler went down Lake Champlain; Schuyler sickened and returned to Albany General Richard Montgomery took the command and at the close of August, he appeared before St.

John on the Sorel, the first military post within
the Canadian lines. He captured the fort and garrison,
and pushing forward, captured Montreal, on
the nothern bank of the St. Lawrence, on the 13th
of November. Flushed with success, he pushed
forward toward his grand destination, Quebec.
He first besieged and then attempted to storm
the city. The attack was unsuccessful, and there
Montgomery lost his life.

[23] In the summer of 1777, Lieutenant-general
Burgoyne, with a large force of British, Germans,
and Canadian soldiers, and a horde of Indians, invaded
New York by the way of Lake Champlain.
He captured Ticonderoga in July, and pressing
forward, reached Saratoga on the upper Hudson,
in September. The Americans fortified Bemis's
Heights near Stillwater, to oppose him. A hard-fought
battle occurred. Burgoyne was driven
back, and after another battle early in October,
he was compelled to surrender his whole force of
more than five thousand men.

[24] Before he crossed the Hudson, a little above
Stillwater, Burgoyne was induced to send an expedition
to Bennington in Vermont, to capture needful
stores and cattle, for his provision had become
very scarce. Five hundred Germans, Canadians,
and Tories, and one hundred Indians, all commanded
by a German officer, composed the expedition.
Colonel John Stark, with the New Hampshire
militia, met them in the town of Hoosick, a

few miles from Bennington, and after a severe engagement, totally routed the invaders. This defeat was a very severe blow to Burgoyne.

[25] The British held possession of a strong fort on Stony Point, a small rocky promontory, jutting into the Hudson river a few miles below the lower entrance to the Highlands. On the night of the 15th July, 1779, General Anthony Wayne led a choice band of soldiers to surprise the garrison. He was entirely successful; and though severely wounded in the head, he wrote to Washington, on the ramparts, at two o'clock in the morning, " The fort and garrison, with Colonel Johnson, are ours." It was one of the most brilliant events of the war.

[26] After being driven before the British host, across New Jersey, Washington and his handful of half-starving, half-naked troops, stood shivering in cold December, on the Pennsylvania shores of the Delaware, opposite Trenton. A detachment of Hessians, under Colonel Rall, occupied that post. Christmas day approached. Washington knew full well that the Germans would have a carouse on that day, and therefore would be weaker and less guarded than usual. On Christmas night he crossed the Delaware in boats, in the midst of floating ice, eight miles above Trenton, and early in the morning, fell upon the Hessians while their commander was yet drinking with boon companions. The Hessians were captured, and were taken across the river as prison-

ers. This bold and brilliant stroke alarmed the British, and gave new courage to the desponding Americans.

[27] Encouraged by his success at Trenton, Washington resolved to act on the offensive. He crossed the Delaware and took post at Trenton. Cornwallis marched against him from Princeton ten miles distant, leaving Colonel Mawhood in command of a detachment there. Cornwallis encamped on one side of a small stream, opposite the American army, on the evening of the 2d of January, 1777, intending to make an easy capture of the "rebels" in the morning. During the night, Washington secretly withdrew; and at dawn, while Cornwallis was rubbing his opening eyelids, he heard the booming of Washington's cannon at Princeton. At first he thought the sound was thunder; he was soon undeceived. The Americans, after a severe skirmish at Princeton, defeated and routed Mawhood, who was greatly applauded for his skill in escaping with two hundred men. Cornwallis came to his assistance, but Washington had hastened forward, and was soon far beyond his reach in the hill-country of the Jerseys.

[28] In September, 1777, the Americans under Washington, had a severe battle with the British under Howe and Cornwallis, on the Brandywine Creek, in lower Pennsylvania, and were defeated with much loss. The British also suffered much loss on that occasion. Not long afterward (early

in October) there was a severe battle at Germantown, in which the Americans and British lost many men; and during that month and November, many more were slain at forts Mifflin and Mercer, on the Delaware, a little below Philadelphia. These events are alluded to by the poet.

²⁹ This phraseology reminds us of the following passage in Milton:

> "Have ye chosen this place,
> After the toils of battle, to repose
> Your wearied virtue; for the ease ye find
> To slumber here, as in the vales of heaven?"

³⁰ See Note 24, Canto II.

³¹ The Scotch Highlanders in North Carolina, already mentioned in Note 14, Canto IV, were generally Loyalists, and at the commencement of 1776, they were organized, enrolled, and armed for the royal cause, under Donald McDonald, who was commissioned a brigadier-general by Martin, the royal governor. McDonald set up his standard at Cross Creek (now Fayetteville), and prepared for conflict. The patriot militia of neighboring districts under Carroll, Moore, and Lillington, marched against them. They met on Moore's Creek, in Hanover county, and on the 27th of February, a severe engagement occurred there. A great many of the Scotchmen were killed, many were made prisoners, and the remainder were

routed and dispersed. Among the prisoners was the husband of Flora McDonald.

[32] In the autumn of 1780, Major Patrick Ferguson, an active officer under Cornwallis, was sent into the mountain districts of South Carolina, to embody the Tories. Early in October, he crossed the Broad River into the Yorkville district, with about fifteen hundred Loyalists, and encamped on King's Mountain. Several corps of Whig militia were united to oppose him, and attacked his camp there on the 7th of October. It was a bloody conflict; Ferguson was killed, and his party were totally defeated, with great loss. This side-engagement was as disastrous to Cornwallis, then marching to invade North Carolina, as was that of Bennington to Burgoyne.

[33] Three months after the victory of the Americans on King's Mountain, General Morgan gained another over Colonel Tarleton at the Cowpens, in the same neighborhood. It was a very brilliant affair, and still more weakened the power of Cornwallis. Tarleton, who was an exceedingly active officer, managed to escape, closely pursued by Colonel William Washington. These two officers had a personal engagement during the pursuit, and Tarleton was wounded in the hand. Afterward, Tarleton was in the company of a witty Whig lady in North Carolina, and remarked in a contemptuous manner, " I would like to see this Colonel Washington of whom you speak so much."

'Had you looked behind you at the battle of the Cowpens, you might have seen him," retorted the lady. Having remarked to her sister, " I understand this Colonel Washington cannot write his name," glancing at Tarleton's scarred hand, the lady instantly replied, " You will acknowledge that he knows how *to make his mark.*"

[34] General Greene, who succeeded General Gates in the command of the Southern Army, was successful during the spring and summer of 1781, in gradually driving the British toward the seaboard. Marching slowly down the Santee, he fell upon the British at Eutaw Springs, on the morning of the 8th of September. A bloody battle ensued, in which neither party gained an absolute victory. It was disastrous to both, but especially so to the British. Although they held the field at the end of the conflict, they immediately abandoned it, and fled percipitately toward Charleston.

[35] Fabius was a successful Roman general, and the great opponent of Hannibal. He was remarkable for his caution. He made many marches and countermarches, and would never be drawn into battle in a disadvantageous position. Because of this system, which in time always worked favorably, he was called " the delayer," and was much censured by the young and reckless officers. Washington pursued a similar course throughout the war, and with the same success; yet he was often censured for his " Fabian slowness."

[36] An English philosophical writer of that name, carried the ideal system of Locke so far as to deny the existence of matter.

[37] This is in allusion to the oft-repeated assertions in parliamentary resolves, in speeches from the throne and the people, and in proclamations, that Britain was *omnipotent*.

[38] These two lines are omitted in the revised editions of 1820; and the last one preceding them was altered so as to read

"Absent from home, or fast asleep?"

[39] The boast of British orators of that day.

[40] Thus British orators and writers alluded to Great Britain oftentimes with much display of pompous declamation.

[41] There was an English ballad, very famous and much sung at that time, in which Neptune (styled *The Watry God*) is made, with great deference, to surrender his trident to King George, and to acknowledge him as monarch and ruler of the ocean. A hundred years before, Waller wrote:

"They that the whole world's monarchy design'd,
Are to their ports by our bold fleet confin'd,
From whence our red cross they triumphant see,
Riding without a rival on the sea."

And again,

"Others may use the ocean as their road,
Only the English make it their abode."

⁴² See Note 47, Canto I.

⁴³ The *Erse* was the ancient language of Scotland. See Note 5, Canto I.

⁴⁴ The old poets aver that Thetis, the mother of Achilles, desirous of making him invulnerable, plunged his whole body into the river Styx (the water that divides mortality from immortality), except his heel, by which she held him. Tradition asserts that he was finally slain by an arrow which penetrated his heel. There are various traditions and myths concerning this celebrated hero of the Trojan War.

⁴⁵ A kibe is a chap or crack occasioned by cold, or an ulcerated chilblain, as in the heels.

⁴⁶ Paris was a son of Priam, king of Troy, and was regarded as the cause of the ruin of his country, as predicted by Æsacus, the soothsayer, at his birth. He seduced and carried to Troy, Helen, the beautiful wife of Menelaus, king of Crete. This outrage led to the siege of Troy, its fall, and the fulfilment of the predictions of Æsacus. Tradition relates that Paris hurled the fatal arrow into the heel of Achilles.

⁴⁷ Job, chapter ii.

⁴⁸ The poet here alludes to the popular scandal concerning the intimacy of General William Howe with the wife of Joshua Loring, the commissary of prisoners, mentioned in Note 91, Canto I. Butler, in his *Hudibras*, says in similar words:

> "The sun had long since, in the lap
> Of Thetis, taken out his nap."

[49] On Sunday evening, March 3, 1776, General Thomas, with two thousand men, and proper entrenching tools, cattle and carts, went secretly to Dorchester Heights (now in South Boston), and there, in the bright moonlight, unobserved by the British in the city, they piled up huge fortifications before the dawn, under the direction of Richard Gridley, a veteran engineer. At break of day, the breastworks were sufficiently high to afford ample protection to the Americans. Howe, overwhelmed with astonishment, exclaimed when he saw those formidable works, "What shall I do? The rebels have done more in one night than my whole army would have done in a month!" They had even done more than pile up the earth—they had placed cannons upon those mounds, and with these commanded the town and harbor of Boston. From that moment, Howe sought means for escape, and finally, through the wisdom and leniency of Washington, he was allowed to sail away for Halifax, unmolested, and followed by more than three thousand Loyalists, who dared not brave the indignation of the victorious Patriots.

[50] The Titans are described by the ancient poets as giants, sons of the earth, who rebelled against Jupiter, the supreme ruler of the universe. They heaped mountains upon mountains, in order to scale Olympus, on whose apex was the throne of Jupiter. They were driven back, discomfited by the thunders of Jove and the arrows of Apollo.

[51] Alluding to the hasty departure of the British from Boston, when Howe perceived that he could no longer keep it. Although Washington had tacitly consented, on the application of Howe, to allow him to depart unmolested, yet great terror pervaded the ranks of the enemy, and the households of the Tories. They all went on board the ships on Sunday morning, March 17th; and on the same day the deserted city was taken possession of by General Putnam in the name of the *Thirteen United Colonies*.

[52] This is an allusion to the cities of refuge among the Jews, in which, if a murderer or other criminal could reach before arrest, he was safe from punishment. The city of refuge here alluded to was Halifax, in Nova Scotia, to which the British army fled.

[53] This was the victorious army of Burgoyne, which, after capturing Ticonderoga and Mount Independence, gained a victory at Hubbardton, and destroyed the American stores at Skenesborough, now Whitehall, at the head of Lake Champlain. Then, flushed with these successes, Burgoyne marched slowly, but unimpeded by American arms through the wilderness toward the Hudson River. The people of that region fled in terror, for they dreaded the savages who accompanied the invaders.

[54] The manner of "hiving" bees, to which this is an allusion, is mentioned in Note 8, Canto I.

[55] The rape of Lucretia, by Sextus Tarquinius,

is given in the old legends as the proximate cause of the downfall of kingly power in Rome. The tragic result of the outrage caused Brutus to swear, by the pure blood which incarnadined a dagger with which Lucretia had stabbed herself, that he would pursue to the uttermost Tarquinius and all his race, and thenceforward suffer no man to be king at Rome. The aroused people gathered together, and passed a decree to the same effect, and Tarquin the Superb was banished. Such is the legend, which sober historians doubt.

[56] See Note 20, Canto III.

[57] This has reference to the death of General Fraser, during the first battle on Bemis's Heights. Fraser was a gallant officer, and was mounted on a splendid iron-gray horse. He was dressed in full uniform, and made a conspicuous mark. Colonel Daniel Morgan, commander of the celebrated rifle corps, perceived that the fate of the battle depended upon Fraser, and he ordered his riflemen to shoot him. As was afterward ascertained, a rifle-ball first cut the crupper of Fraser's horse, and soon another passed through his horse's mane. Fraser's aid noticed it and said, "It is evident that you are marked out for particular aim; would it not be prudent for you to retire from this place?" Fraser replied, "My duty forbids me to fly from danger;" and the next moment he fell, mortally wounded by a ball from the rifle of Timothy Mur-

phy, one of Morgan's men, who took sure aim from a small tree into which he had mounted.

[58] "Loose his beard and hoary hair,
  Streamed like a meteor to the troubled air."—GRAY.

[59] Judges xv. 15.

[60] After Burgoyne had surrendered his army at Saratoga, and the terms of the capitulation were agreed upon and settled, the prisoners, English and Hessian, started under guard across the country to Cambridge. They commenced the march to the tune of Yankee Doodle, which they had so often heard in derision in the British camp. The pride of Burgoyne was dreadfully humbled by the whole affair. He had declared that he would eat his Christmas dinner in Albany, as a victor. He dined there sooner than Christmas, but as a prisoner, although a guest at the table of General Schuyler, whom he had greatly injured, by causing his house, mills, and other property at Saratoga, to be burned.

[61] This allusion to Burgoyne's foppery is a very happy one, as the young men of fashion who composed the *Macaroni Club* had very recently produced a great sensation in England. They were young men who had travelled in Italy, and had returned, bringing with them all the vices and follies which they had picked up there. They formed their club in London in 1772, and were particularly distinguished for their extravagance

in dress. They wore enormous knots of hair behind, an exceedingly small cocked hat, an enormous walking-stick with long tassels, and jacket, waistcoat, and breeches, cut very close. Soon every thing that was fashionable was *à la Macaroni*. Macaroni articles everywhere abounded, and Macaroni songs were set to Macaroni music. One song closed with this stanza:

> " Five pounds of hair they wear behind,
>   The ladies to delight, O,
> Their senses give unto the wind,
>   To make themselves a fright, O.
> The fashion who does e'er pursue,
>   I think a simple-toney;
> For he's a fool, say what you will,
>   Who is a Macaroni."

The word *macaroni* took the place of *beau* and *fribble*, which had been given previously to men of fashion.

⁶² See Note 66, Canto II. Bellona was the accomplished goddess of war.

⁶³ General Burgoyne was a natural son of Lord Bingley, and was not only a successful soldier, but a polished gentleman. He was a brigadier in Portugal in 1762. He was afterward a privy councillor, and when he came to America in 1775, and while a prisoner of war in 1777, he was a member of the British Parliament. His misfortunes here deprived him of the sunshine of the royal countenance; and in 1780, after publishing his vindica-

tion, he resigned all offices and their emoluments and in 1781 joined the opposition in Parliament, in favor of the Americans. From that time until his death, in August, 1792, he was chiefly employed in literary pursuits, in which he delighted.

[64] When setting out for America, Burgoyne playfully remarked that he meant to dance the Whig ladies to obedience, and their husbands would soon follow In this, as in many other things, the British officers were disappointed. Howe and Clinton, and some of their subordinates, expected to "crush the rebellion" in a week almost; and they actually brought fishing-tackle with them, to have some fine sport after the smoke of gunpowder had cleared away.

[65] Burgoyne's proclamations, like those of Gage, were very pompous. He was fond of making them, for he always delighted in the use of his pen. While in Boston, during the siege, he wrote a farce called *Boston Blockaded*, in which the person designed to represent Washington enters with uncouth gait, wearing a large wig, a long, rusty sword, and attended by a country servant with a rusty gun. Other American officers were similarly burlesqued. While this farce was in course of performance in the temporary theatre in Boston, on the night of the 8th of January, 1776, a sergeant suddenly entered and exclaimed, "The Yankees are attacking our works on Bunker's Hill!" The audience thought this was part of

the play, and laughed immoderately at the idea ; but they were soon undeceived by the burly voice of Howe shouting, " Officers, to your alarm-posts ! " The people were dispersed in great confusion. The fact was, that Majors Knowlton, Carey, and Henly, three gallant American officers, had crossed the mill-dam from Cobble Hill, and had set fire to some houses in Charlestown, at the foot of Bunker's Hill, occupied by some British soldiers. They burned eight houses, killed one man, and carried off five prisoners.

[66] Matthew Prior wrote his *Alma*, the best of his works, while in confinement in the Tower of London.

[67] Sir Walter Raleigh wrote his famous *History of the World*, while confined in the Tower on a charge of treason. The first volume appeared in 1614.

[68] John Wilkes, already mentioned in Note 88, Canto III, was a fearless political writer during the early years of the reign of George the Third, and for a long time he was editor of *The North Britain*. In the 45th number of that paper, published in 1763, he uttered sentiments considered libellous, and he was sent to the Tower. His arrest was proved to be illegal, and he was released. For several years, as editor, as alderman in London, and as a member of the House of Commons, he was considered a very dangerous enemy to the crown. Wilkes was a licentious, unprincipled

man; and because he wrote an indecent *Essay on Woman*, he was arraigned before the King's Bench, and, upon conviction, was expelled from Parliament. He afterward obtained a verdict against Wood, the under-secretary of state, with $5,000 damages, and soon went to Paris He returned to England, was elected to the House of Commons in 1768, but was deprived of his seat. He became Lord Mayor of London in 1774, when he took his seat in the House of Commons, and was the friend of the Americans. He was afterward Chamberlain of London. Wilkes flourished but in the midst of agitation. When out of the troubled sea of politics, he sunk into obscurity, and died in the Isle of Wight, in 1797, at the age of 70 years.

[69] General Prescott was twice made prisoner, during the Revolution. The first time he was captured at Montreal by Montgomery, near the close of 1775; and the second time he was seized in his rooms, while in command of the British on Rhode Island, in July, 1777, taken to the Head-Quarters of the American army, and afterward exchanged for General Charles Lee, who had been captured in New Jersey in December previous. Colonel William Barton, with a few men in whale-boats, crossed Narragansett Bay in the night, for the purpose of seizing Prescott, who was a petty tyrant of the meanest stamp. He was taken from his bedroom, conveyed across to Warwick, and from

thence to Providence, and afterward to Head-Quarters. A full account of the affair, with a portrait of Barton and a picture of the house from which Prescott was taken, may be found in Lossing's *Pictorial Field Book of the Revolution.*

[70] Here again is an allusion to Burgoyne's farce of *The Siege of Boston.* The *Maid of the Oaks* was another farce from his pen, which was much thought of, and was often performed in the English theatres. He also wrote a comedy entitled *The Heiress*, which had great reputation. Some critics have pronounced it one of the best productions of the modern British drama.

[71] This refers to the cruelties toward prisoners, charged to Joshua Loring, the commissary. If the stories related of his inhumanity to those who fell into his hands were true, he was even worse than the detested Cunningham, the keeper of the Provost prison in New York. The Vampyre was a creation of superstition, a belief in which prevailed extensively among many nations in Europe. It was pretended to be a dead body, which arose from the grave at night, and sucked the blood of the living.

[72]
"a place
Before his eyes appeared, sad, noisome, dark,
A Lazar-house it seemed ―― Despair
Tended the sick, busiest from couch to couch,
And over them triumphant Death his dart
Shook, but delayed to strike."
Milton's *Paradise Lost*, Book XI.

[73] *Murder* was thus spelled in former times.

[74] Sir Guy Carleton was a very humane man After the unfortunate attack of the Americans on Quebec, at the close of 1775, he treated the "rebel" prisoners with great humanity, and finally paroled them.

[75] It has been asserted, and not denied, that after the battle near Brooklyn, on Long Island, Howe and Clinton both allowed their troops, and especially the Hessians, to tie up American prisoners and use them for marks to fire at. The excuse was that such treatment would keep the people from joining the rebel army, and thus the rebellion would be sooner ended!"

[76] Among other measures to distress the people, great pains were taken by the British in New York, to communicate the small-pox throughout the country, and especially to the American army. At that time Jenner had just announced, in England, his great discovery of *vaccination*, but it was not practised in America until about the close of the Revolution. *Inoculation* was resorted to; and while the army lay in the Highlands in 1781 the soldiers were inoculated by companies.

[77] After the battles on Long Island and Fort Washington, where a great many Americans were made prisoners, the places of confinement on shipboard and in New York were crowded with the captives. Impure air and food soon caused a terrible mortality among them. They died by

scores, and the disease known as the prison-fever, similar to that of the ship fever of our day, became apparently contagious. The British endeavored to infect the American camp with the disease. A multitude of Americans perished on board the old *Jersey* and other prison-ships in the harbor of New York, and in the old sugar-houses in the city, which, being strong and large, were converted into jails.

[78] Judges, Chapter iv.

[79] *Punic* was the ancient language of the Carthaginians; and the contests in which the Romans and that people were involved, during more than three centuries, were called Punic Wars. The Carthaginians were so notoriously treacherous, and unfaithful, that the Romans made the expression *Punica Fides*—Punic Faith—synonymous with unfaithfulness to promises.

[80] Ammon or Hammon was the name given to Jupiter, as worshipped in Libya, in Africa. He is represented with the head and horns of a ram, because a legend asserts that when the army under Bacchus was in Africa, and about to perish for want of water, a ram appeared and guided them to an oasis where it was found in abundance. Bacchus erected a temple to Jupiter on the spot, and gave the impersonation of the deity the form above mentioned. The poet thought Loring a fit priest, because (again alluding to the unfaithfulness of the commissary's wife) the Libyan Ammon wore horns.

[81] *Bel* or *Baal* was an ancient Chaldean idol, mentioned by both Isaiah and Jeremiah. Baal is also mentioned in the Book of Numbers, Judges, and Kings. It is said to have devoured enormous quantities of food daily, which the people supplied, and which, of course, the priests and their friends consumed.

[82] Moloch was the chief idol of the Ammonites, in Canaan, and is mentioned in the eleventh chapter of 1 Kings. The idol was made of brass, seated on a throne of the same metal, with the head of a calf, and a crown on it. Parents often sacrificed their children to this divinity. It was heated by fire beneath, and when the children were put into its hot brazen arms, they rolled into the idol and were consumed. Bullocks and other animals were also offered to Moloch in sacrifice.

[83] See Rabelais's history of the Giant *Gargantua*.

[84] Jonah, Chapter i.

[85] Genesis, Chapter xli.

[86] This sentence refers to the alleged cruelties of Lord Clive (who was governor first of Fort St. David, and then of Bengal in the East Indies) toward the native inhabitants, whom, as military commander, he conquered. By his exploits he gained the title of Omrah of the Mogul Empire, an Irish peerage and immense wealth. He retired to England in 1767, and in November, 1773, he committed suicide by cutting his throat. The

"Black Hole" referred to, was a dungeon in Calcutta, where, on the 20th of June, 1756, the Nabob or chief man confined one hundred and forty-six British gentlemen—merchants and others in the service of the East India Company, in a room only eighteen feet square. The heat, crushing, and stench of the dungeon, caused the death of one hundred and twenty-three of the prisoners before morning. It was the Provost prison (now Hall of Records) in New York, and especially the sugar house in Liberty street, and the Jersey prison ship, which the poet here alludes to in the comparison.

[67] The various districts of the East Indies were governed by wealthy subordinate rulers called Nabobs. It has become a term significant of a very wealthy man.

[83] In the latter part of his life Lord Clive conceived himself haunted by the ghosts of those persons in the East, who were the victims of his inhumanity. Notwithstanding the alleged cruelties of Clive were not doubted by the British nation, the then corrupt Parliament, before whom he was accused, awarded him a vote of thanks for his services in the East Indies. But

"Conscience makes cowards of us all."

[89] These three commanders were famous during portions of the war, for their marauding services.

[90] Judges, Chapter xv.

[91] We have already referred to the ravages of Tryon and others on the New England coasts, and to the operations of Lord Dunmore in Virginia. In South Carolina, likewise, many negroes were taken from the plantations, by marauding parties, and those who did not perish were sent to the West Indies and sold. And every where, especially during the earlier years of the war, before the opportunities which the Americans obtained for retaliation had taught the British and Hessian troops circumspection, they committed the most outrageous crimes.

[92] The King and Parliament were both long deceived by the reports of expected aids from the Tories sent over by the military commanders here. Indeed, it was believed by the ministry, even as late as the time of the capture of Burgoyne, that the whig party was a very small one, and that the great body of the people of the colonies were loyal, when fear of the violent patriots would allow them to be so. The fact was the reverse of this.

[93] In February, 1778, Lord North proposed in parliament, a conciliatory plan, which, he thought, would end all difficulties with the colonies. He proposed to repeal all obnoxious acts of parliament, if the Americans would rescind their Declaration of Independence, and return to the loyalty of loving colonists. The proposition was in the form of two bills. These bills arrived in America about the middle of April. They were looked

upon with suspicion, and were called "deceptionary bills." Congress refused to accede to the terms offered in these bills, because the independence of the colonies was not guarantied. Commissioners to negotiate with Congress, in accordance with North's proposition, arrived in June. They were the Earl of Carlisle, George Johnstone, formerly governor of West Florida, and William Eden, a brother of the then late governor of Maryland. They were accompanied by the eminent Adam Ferguson, as secretary. The proceedings of Congress, before the arrival of the Commissioners, had barred the door effectually to all negotiations, and they found their "occupation gone."

[94] ———— " medicatam frugibus offam." See an account of the descent of Æneas into hell, in Virgil's Æneid, Book vi.

[95] When the commissioners found they could do nothing officially, Johnstone determined to try the power of money and place, by offering such bribes to public men. Because of his notoriously corrupt conduct, the Congress declared that no intercourse should be had with him. Yet he persisted, flattering some and boldly approaching others with promises of royal favor.

[96] The "petticoated politician" here alluded to, was an American lady, daughter of Dr. Thomas Graeme of Pennsylvania, and then the wife of Hugh Ferguson, a relation of the secretary of the

commissioner. Her husband being in the British service, she was much in the company of Loyalists. Being a woman of superior attainments, and acquainted with many leading men in Congress, Johnstone succeeded in making her an unconscious instrument of his corrupt efforts. He first spoke to her warmly in favor of American interests, and she believed him to be a true friend of her country. He expressed a strong desire to stop the effusion of blood, and intimated that, if a proper representation could be made to leading men in Congress, a reconciliation might yet be effected. Her womanly sympathies were aroused, and Johnstone, who was not permitted to go within the American lines, desired Mrs. Ferguson to say to General Joseph Reed that, provided he could, conformably to his conscience and views of things, exert his influence to settle the dispute, he might command ten thousand guineas and the best post in government. Mrs. Ferguson suggested that such a proposition would be considered as a bribe by General Reed. Johnstone disclaimed the idea; and, convinced of his sincerity and good will, she sought an interview with General Reed, three days after the British evacuated Philadelphia, and laid the proposition before him. Reed afterward declared, that he at once exclaimed, "My influence is but small, but were it as great as Governor Johnstone would insinuate, the King of Great Britain has nothing within his gift that would tempt me."

This attempt at bribery was soon made known to the public. The alleged reply of General Reed went from lip to lip; the commissioners were every where denounced, and poor Mrs. Ferguson, the innocent dupe of a corrupt hireling, was accused of being a British emissary. She outlived all suspicions, however.

[97] Benedict Arnold's services against his government were actually purchased for ten thousand guineas and the commission of a brigadier in the British army. This was the stipulated consideration for the betrayal of the strong fortress at West Point and its dependencies, into the hands of Sir Henry Clinton, in September, 1780. He failed in his wicked purpose, escaped to the enemy, received his reward, and performed eminent marauding services for his royal master, during the remainder of the war. Arnold had been a brave, skilful, and exceedingly useful officer before his fall.

[98] It was very fortunate for the Americans, that inefficient men like the brothers Howe commanded the British land and naval forces at the commencement of the Revolution. General Howe, in particular, always moved slowly, and when he had gained a victory, he almost always lost the advantages of it by supineness. Such was the case after his victory near Brooklyn. The really captive army of Washington within the American lines escaped to New York, while Howe was sleeping

and yet, for his *victory* on that occasion, he was knighted and became Sir William Howe. He remained in Philadelphia after he had captured it in the autumn of 1777, for many months, with a well-provisioned and well-furnished army, while the half-starved, half-clad, and feeble force of the Americans were shivering and famishing at Valley Forge, only twenty miles distant. Yet he made no attempt at what might have been an easy capture of the whole. His idle army in the city became greatly weakened by inactivity and dissipation. Dr. Franklin justly observed, " Howe has not taken Philadelphia; Philadelphia has taken Howe." The acute Colonel Hamilton, young as he was, said to General Washington, when that officer was regretting his failure in capturing Howe,—" For my part I am glad of it, for Great Britain might have sent a more active man in his place."

[99] The Continental Congress held its session at York, Pennsylvania, while the British held possession of Philadelphia during the winter and spring of 1778. In May, after being honored by a remarkable *fête* called *Mischianza*, in the preparation of which the unfortunate Major André was the principal actor, General Howe resigned the command of the army to Sir Henry Clinton and returned to England. He was severely censured by Burgoyne and other military men, and some spicy correspondence, statements, &c., ensued.

Howe was a good-natured, full-fed, heavy, indolent man—" the most indolent of mortals," according to General Charles Lee, who averred that he " never took pains to examine the merits or demerits of the cause in which he was engaged." Howe published a narrative of his campaigns in America, the style of which partakes largely of the sluggishness of his character. He died in 1814.

[100] This was Sir Henry Clinton. He was grandson of Francis, sixth Earl of Lincoln, and was Knight of the Bath. He came to America just before the Battle of Bunker Hill, and remained until near the close of the war. Clinton was quite an active officer, yet not a very skilful one. Soon after his return home, he published a narrative of his campaigns in 1781–83, which Lord Cornwallis, another of the British commanders here, thought it necessary to answer. To this Clinton made a reply. Clinton was Governor of Gibraltar in 1795, and the same year he was elected a member of parliament. He died the following year.

[101] Soon after taking command of the British army in America, Sir Henry Clinton was informed that a powerful French fleet, under the Count D'Estaing, was on its way, and would probably block up and perhaps capture the British vessels in the Delaware under the command of Earl Howe, and thus secure New York. He immediately resolved to evacuate Philadelphia and the

Delaware, and hasten with army and fleet to New York. With eleven thousand men and an immense baggage and provision train he started for New York, by way of New Brunswick. Washington, at Valley Forge, was on the alert, and commenced a pursuit of Clinton with a more than equal force. By the adroit movement of detachments, he compelled Clinton to change his course in the direction of Sandy Hook.

[102] Clinton was sore pressed by his pursuers, and the New Jersey militia greatly annoyed him on the flanks. Finally he was obliged to halt at Monmouth Court-House, (now Freehold, New Jersey,) change front, and engage in a general battle with the Americans. The engagement commenced quite early on Sunday morning, the 28th day of June, 1778. It was one of the hottest days ever experienced in that latitude. All day the conflict raged, and night only put an end to it. Both parties slept on their arms, the Americans, under Washington, intending to renew the battle in the morning. Clinton chose rather to avoid that necessity, and at midnight he silently resumed his march, undiscovered by the wearied and sleeping Americans.

[103] In his official dispatch to Lord George Germain, Clinton wrote: " Having reposed the troops until ten at night, to avoid the excessive heat of the day, I took advantage of the moonlight to rejoin General Knyphausen, [the commander of the

Hessians,] who had advanced to Nut Swamp, near Middletown." This dispatch caused a great deal of merriment in America, for it was known that the event took place at about the time of new moon. *Poor Will's Almanac*, printed by Joseph Cruikshank, in Philadelphia, indicates the occurrence of new moon, on the 24th of June, and being four days old on the night of the battle, it set at fifty-five minutes past ten. Clinton had waited for its setting in order to

"Steal off on tiptoe in the dark."

[104] In his retreat, Clinton placed Knyphausen and his Germans in the rear. In fact during the whole time of service of the German troops in America, they were always used as shields to the British, and were made to perform those services in which honorable soldiers would not willingly consent to be engaged.

[105] The poet's allusion here, to the remarkable event recorded in the tenth chapter of the Book of Joshua, is very pertinent, and is elucidated by note 103.

[106] This refers to the treaty of friendship and alliance, formed between the struggling colonies and France, on the 6th of February, 1778. The Bourbon king of France had been secretly aiding the revolted colonies, by supplies of arms, ammunition, and money, ever since 1776, but unwilling to have an untimely rupture with Great Britain,

all the transactions were so conducted as to have a commercial aspect in private hands. But when the success of the Americans appeared certain after they had, unaided, captured the powerful army of Burgoyne, the French king saw that he might then inflict a severe blow upon his old enemy, England, by acknowledging the independence of the colonies, and by forming an alliance with them. That measure was soon accomplished, and the intelligence that, on account of that alliance, France had sent a powerful fleet to America, caused, as we have seen (note 101), the evacuation of Philadelphia and the Delaware by the British land and naval forces.

[107] Pursuant to the terms of the treaty of alliance with France, the Count D'Estaing sailed from Toulon with a powerful fleet in April, 1778, and arrived off the Capes of the Delaware in July following. The British fleet had escaped to the safe anchorage within Sandy Hook, where the heavy French vessels could not reach them. After blockading Howe's fleet there for a short time, D'Estaing sailed eastward, to aid the Americans in rescuing Rhode Island from the British. Off Newport, in August, D'Estaing and a fleet under Howe, which had followed him from New York, attempted to fight, but a terrible gale dispersed both fleets, and damaged them badly.

[108] In 1779, D'Estaing was sent to the West Indies with a powerful fleet, captured St. Vincent

and Grenada from the English, defeated Admiral Biron in a naval engagement, and made prizes of a British ship-of-the-line, and several frigates, on the southern coast of the United States. He also assisted in the siege of Savannah, in the autumn of that year; but, pretending to fear the effect of the autumn storms upon his fleet, he abandoned the siege when victory was almost in the grasp of the allies, and went to sea.

[109] Charles Henry, Count D'Estaing, was a native of Auvergne, France. He was a famous soldier in the French service in the East Indies in 1756, was made prisoner by the English, broke his parole and escaped. He commanded an expedition against Grenada. He became a member of the Assembly of Notables in the French Revolution, and, being suspected of unfriendliness toward the Terrorists, he was guillotined in April, 1793.

[110] Francis Joseph Paul, Count De Grasse, was a native of France, and born in 1723. He was an active naval officer in the West Indies, before coming upon the American coast, and afterward performed signal service in assisting in the capture of Cornwallis and his army at Yorktown in October, 1781. He formed an alliance with an unworthy woman after his return to France, whose conduct embittered his life. He died early in 1788, at the age of sixty-five years.

[111] The life and services of the Marquis De La

Fayette, are too well known to every American reader, to need any special notice here.

[112] General Lincoln was second in command of the army under Gates, at the capture of Burgoyne. He was appointed to succeed General Robert Howe in command of the southern army, in 1779; and in the spring of 1780, having been ordered by Congress to defend Charleston, the capital of South Carolina, at all hazards, he collected what force he could there, and sustained a siege, conducted by Sir Henry Clinton, Lord Cornwallis, and Admiral Arbuthnot, for several weeks. He was at length compelled to yield, and on the 12th of May surrendered his army and the city to the victorious enemy.

[113] After the capture of Charleston, the British officers displayed an activity hitherto unknown to them, and Clinton left Cornwallis to take energetic measures for a complete subjugation of the whole South. Cornwallis himself marched up the Santee toward Camden; another detachment under Colonel Cruger took possession of Fort Ninety-six in the south-western part of South Carolina, and another, under Lieutenant-colonel Brown, who, like Cruger, was an American Loyalist, took possession of Augusta, in Georgia. For a while, these two States were completely crushed beneath the heel of British power.

[114] This refers to the partisan corps under Sumter, Morgan, Marion, Pickens, Clark, Buford,

and other bold leaders, but especially to the vanquished army of Gates mentioned in the next note.

[115] General Gates was sent to the South after the fall of Charleston, to rally the patriots and reclaim Georgia and South Carolina. He went with proud confidence of success, and in a night and early morning, engagement with Cornwallis, near Camden, he was signally defeated, his whole army was dispersed, and he was compelled to become a flying fugitive with only a handful of attendants. General Charles Lee, (then in disgrace because of bad conduct at Monmouth,) who knew Gates well, said to him, on his departure, " Take care that you do not exchange your Northern laurels for Southern willows." To this the poet alludes.

[116] After the defeat of Gates, Cornwallis pressed forward into North Carolina, took post at Hillsborough, and really held military sway, even to the borders of Virginia, which, also, he included in his programme of conquest.

[117] This is in allusion to Arnold's marauding expeditions in Virginia. He sent off several cargoes of negroes and tobacco (the fruits of his plunder) to the West Indies, and sold them for his own profit.

[118] Admiral Lord Rodney, having been unsuccessful in attempting to recapture St. Vincent from the French, in 1781, sailed for the Dutch

island of St. Eustatius, where there was an immense amount of goods, belonging to people of several nations, neutrals as well as belligerents, because it was a free island. The Governor had not heard of the commencement of hostilities between Great Britain and Holland, and being unprepared, made no defence. The value of the capture was immense. Two hundred and fifty vessels, some with rich cargoes, were taken, and goods valued at three millions of pounds sterling were seized. This capture of property belonging to subjects of neutral nations, and the general seizure and sale of private as well as public property for the benefit of the captors, was truly an insult to the laws of nations.

[119] In allusion to Tryon's marauding expeditions already referred to.

[120] After the defeat of Gates near Camden, in August, 1780, General Nathaniel Greene was appointed to the command of the Southern army. He soon gathered a considerable force, took post at Cheraw on the east, and on the Broad River on the west, and prepared to reclaim the Carolinas. He was, however, compelled to flee before Cornwallis to Virginia, early in 1781. Greene remained in Virginia only long enough to refresh his troops and receive recruits, when he again entered North Carolina. The decisive battle at Guilford Court-House, in which Cornwallis was victor, so far as maintaining the field was con-

cerned, occurred in March. "Another such vie tory," said Charles Fox in the House of Commons, "will ruin the British army." It was disastrous to Cornwallis, and he hastened with the remains of his army to Wilmington, near the seaboard, and then pushed forward into Virginia, where Benedict Arnold, the traitor, was marauding.

[121] During the spring and summer of 1781, Greene swept every vestige of British power from the interior of the Carolinas, and drove the enemy toward the coast. Outposts, forts, encampments, depots, all were captured or broken up, and the lost South was almost completely regained. When, in October, Cornwallis surrendered at Yorktown, the British in South Carolina were confined to Charleston, and those in Georgia were hemmed within the narrow limits of Savannah and its immediate vicinity.

[122] After in vain attempting to overrun and subdue Virginia, Cornwallis, close pressed by La Fayette, Wayne and Steuben, slowly retired seaward; and, pursuant to orders from General Clinton, to be prepared to come to his aid at New York, if necessary, he crossed the James River and took post at Portsmouth, opposite Norfolk. Disl king that situation, he entered the Chesapeake Bay, and going up York River, commenced fortifying the village of York, and Gloucester Point, opposite. There he constructed heavy fortifications, and seemed to defy the power of the Americans.

[123] When General Clinton heard of the march of the allied armies southward, he sent Admiral Graves to assist Cornwallis. But the Count De Grasse, who had just arrived with his fleet from the West Indies, was already in Lynn Haven Bay, within the capes, and Graves could not enter York River. After the two fleets had a slight combat just outside the mouth of the Chesapeake, Graves withdrew.

[124] Count Rochambeau, the commander-in-chief of the French army in America, joined Washington on the Hudson, a few miles above New York, in the summer of 1781. After deceiving Clinton into the belief that they intended to attack him in New York, the allied armies made rapid marches southward, at the suggestion of La Fayette, who was watching Cornwallis there. They arrived at Williamsburgh, a few miles from Yorktown, twelve thousand strong, on the 28th of September, and made immediate preparations to attack the invader.

[125] After the capture of Burgoyne at Saratoga, in 1777, to *Burgoyne an army*, was a favorite expression in America, when alluding to a total and complete capture.

[126] According to Ovid, in his Metamorphoses, Cadmus, the founder of Grecian Thebes, wishing to sacrifice to the gods a cow which he had followed to the spot, by command of the Delphic Oracle, he sent to a fountain for water. It was

guarded by a serpent, which he afterwards killed. By direction of Minerva, he sowed its teeth, and instantly a crop of armed men started up from the ground, five of whom assisted him in building Thebes.

[127] Finding his fortifications to be gradually crumbling under the terrible blows of the allied besiegers, Cornwallis sought shelter for himself and army, by flight. He determined to cross the York river, break through the French troops on the other side, and make forced marches toward New York. Just as a part of his troops were embarked a sudden tempest arose, and they were driven back. Cornwallis was foiled, and saw no alternative but surrender or destruction.

[128] Yorktown stands upon a high bluff of rock marl, making the shore of the York river, very precipitous. At the foot of this bank Cornwallis had an excavation made, in which, secure from the rage of battle above, he held councils with his officers. That excavation has now disappeared, but another made since, was shown to visitors, at a shilling a-piece, as the identical one, when the writer visited Yorktown a few years ago.

[129] Driven to extremities, and despairing of aid from General Clinton, Cornwallis offered to negotiate for a surrender of his whole army. It was done, and in the presence of a vast concourse of people assembled from the country, and before the allied armies, the sword of Cornwallis was

delivered by General O'Hara to General Lincoln, and the whole army laid down their arms, on the 19th of October, 1781. The shipping in the river—every thing—became spoils of victory. The whole number of persons surrendered, was a little more than seven thousand.

[130] The Virginia Loyalists, and those who had accompanied Cornwallis from North Carolina.

[131] Edicts issued by the popes were called Bulls, from the seal (*bulla*) attached to them. These seals were made of metals and wax. The celebrated " golden *bull* " of the Emperor Charles the Fourth, was so called because the seal was made of gold.

[132] The British commanders, and especially Cornwallis, had proclaimed full protection to the Loyalists, on all occasions. There were about fifteen hundred Tories with Cornwallis at Yorktown. All the favor he asked for them, on his surrender, was that a vessel might be provided to carry away the most obnoxious, who were afraid to meet the resentment of the Whigs.

[133] Genesis, Chapter iv.

[134]
> "From his horrid hair,
> Shakes pestilence and war."
>
> *Milton.*

[135] We have before alluded to the often repeated assurances in British proclamations, that

the "door of mercy is now open," and "the door of mercy will be shut." The poet seemed to fear that the hinge of that door so constantly swinging, might be quite worn out.

[136] The genius of America was generally represented as a native female, in the scant costume of the aborigines, and head dressed with the long plumage of the eagle and other birds. Such a figure may be seen on the colonial pendant seals. "Tories dressed in plumes," is an allusion to their being tarred and feathered.

[137] Referring to the American flag.

[138] In allusion to Lord Mansfield's favorite disposition of culprits, by transporting them into exile in some colony of Great Britain.

[139] King George the Third, and Lord North, his prime minister.

[140] In law, a writ to restrain a person from going out of the kingdom, without the king's permission.

[141] The description of Continental paper money, which here follows, is one of the finest examples of the sublime burlesque to be found in our language, especially when all its allusions are made plain by the light of history.

[142] The crutches called "Regulation" and "Tender," by which the specter was supported, were the acts of the State legislatures, in their attempts to prevent the depreciation of the Continental money, and to maintain its credit. Some of those acts

were for the *regulation* of the prices of commodities, and the others were to make that paper a lawful *tender*, in payment for goods, or debts.

[143] On all the emissions of Continental Bills, there was printed the pledge of Congress for their punctual redemption, in the words, " The Faith of the United States."

[144] See Note 62, Canto IV.

[145] On the 22d of June, 1775, the Continental Congress resolved to issue bills of credit, or paper money, to pay the current expenses of the war. This was called *Continental money.* These bills were issued soon afterward, and new emissions were authorized from time to time, until the aggregate sum put forth represented two hundred millions of dollars. Within a little more than two years after their emission, they began to depreciate in value, because the pledge, printed upon each bill, that Congress would pay gold and silver for them, could not be redeemed. In 1780, forty paper dollars were worth only one in specie; and so rapid was the depreciation, that at the close of 1781, they were worthless. They had performed a temporary public good, but produced much inconvenience, and even suffering, to individuals. To the worthlessness of this currency the poet alludes in speaking of the "Ghost of Continental money."

[146] Brazil in South America, is one of the chief sources from whence diamonds have been pro-

cured in modern times. The allusion to Peruvian wealth, refers to the rich gold and silver mines—the richest then known in the world—discovered by the Spanish conquerors of Peru, as well as the immense amount of precious metals found in the temples, and in the palaces of the Incas or rulers of that country.

[147] Danæ was the daughter of a king of Argos, who on consulting an oracle, was told that she would bear a son who would deprive the king of his life. To prevent this, the king shut her up in a brazen tower, with her nurse. Jupiter had seen and loved the maiden; and under the form of a golden shower, he poured through the roof, into her bosom. She became the mother of Perseus, by Jupiter, and the young man killed his grandfather, by accident.

[148] One of the most ruinous speculations of modern times, was the conception of John Law of Edinburgh, who, by remarkable shrewdness in financial schemes, became comptroller-general of the treasury of France. He proposed three schemes—a bank, an East India Company, and a Mississippi Land and Trading Company. The French ministry became enamored with his plans in 1710, and in 1716 Law opened a bank in his own name, under the Regent of France. Most of the people of property, and of all ranks, purchased shares in his bank and his companies, with the expectation of immense profits. His was de

clared a royal bank in 1718. The shares rapidly appreciated in value—upwards of twenty-fold that of the original—and in 1719, they were worth eighty times the amount of all the current specie in France. That great fabric of false credit fell to the ground the following year, and almost prostrated the French government in its fall. Tens of thousands of families were utterly ruined.

[140] It is a singular fact that a scheme of speculation similar to that of Law's in France, had birth in England the same year (1710), and exploded the same year (1720). A company was incorporated in 1716, under the name of the *South Sea Company*. The affair promised immense gains to the stockholders, and the shares, originally £100, raised to the enormous price of £1000! As in France, almost every person of wealth in Great Britain, became stockjobbers and speculators in the fatal scheme. The airy fabric fell in 1720, and ruined thousands of families. The estates of the directors, valued at £2,014,000, were seized in 1721. Mr. Knight, the cashier, absconded with £100,000, but compounded for £10,000, and returned. The success of Law's scheme in France, was the origin of the similar scheme in England. The papers and pamphlets of the time, contained many squibs during the prevalence of the mania, and after the bubble burst, caricatures in abundance appeared, in ridicule of the whole thing. "Bubble-Cards" were used

by players, all bearing some appropriate verse. give one as a fair specimen:

> "A lady pawns her jewels by her maid,
> And in declining stock presumes to trade,
> Till in South Sea at length she drowns her coin,
> And now in Bristol stones glad is to shine."

[150] The infancy of modern chemistry, assumed the charlatan form of Alchemy, or the pretence of transmuting baser metals into gold. It was pretended that a certain powder, known to chemists, would convert base metals into gold; and many men have wasted their lives in attempts to discover this philosopher's stone, as that powder was called. At about 1782, Dr. Price, of Guilford, England, professed to have made the discovery, and carried specimens of his gold to the king, affirming that it was made by means of a red and white powder. He was a Fellow of the Royal Society, and was required, on pain of expulsion, to repeat his experiments before a committee of that body. After some equivocation, he committed suicide by the use of poison, in 1783. The Philosopher's stone may be ranked with Perpetual motion, the Inextinguishable lamp, the Quadrature of the circle, and other impossibilities, which have puzzled and deranged the brains of otherwise sensible men.

[151] The name of Midas appears among the earliest mythological legends of the Greeks, as king

of a district in Thrace. One legend (to which our poet here refers), represents Midas as having on one occasion excited the gratitude of Bacchus, who desired him to ask any favor he pleased. Midas requested that whatever he touched might be turned to gold. It was granted. The myth doubtless illustrates the historical fact of an ancient Phrygian prince, who became very wealthy by mines and by commercial operations.

[152] The Continental money, as here indicated, performed a vast amount of public good, during the first years of the war, notwithstanding its depreciation, as we have said, fell heavily upon the great mass of the people. It carried on the financial operations of the war; and weak and faithless as it afterwards proved, it was the very sinews of strength in providing means for opposing the superior power of Great Britain, in the conflict.

[153] In order to facilitate the depreciation of Continental paper money, and thus weaken this arm of patriotic resistance, vast quantities of counterfeit Continental bills were printed, and sent into the country from New York and Long Island. In Gaine's *New York Mercury*, April 14th, 1777, appeared the following significant advertisement: " Persons going into other colonies may be supplied with any number of counterfeited Congress notes, for the price of the paper per ream. They are so neatly and exactly executed, that there is no risk in getting them off, being almost

impossible to discover that they are not genuine. This has been proven by bills to a very large amount which have already been successfully circulated. Inquire of Q. E. D. at the coffee-house, from 11 A. M. to 5 P. M. during the present month." These counterfeits were sent into the country by cart-loads. Such was one of the dishonorable modes of warfare, employed by the British commanders here. The younger Pitt, when prime minister of England, caused a large number of French assignats to be forged at Birmingham, to depreciate the currency of the French republic. Napoleon also caused forged notes of the Austrian Bank to be distributed throughout the Austrian Tyrol.

[154] Exodus, Chapter viii, verse 17.

[155] Portions of the shores of Great Britain are remarkable for cliffs of chalk, which may be seen at a great distance. For this reason, Cæsar gave it the name of *Albion*.

[6] The common penalty for felony in England, was transportation to the colonies, and many left their country for their country's good. The idea of transporting the whole Island, was a grand amplification in the mind of the poet.

[157] The superficial area of Lake Erie is greater than that of England; while Lake Superior, the largest body of fresh water in the world, is twenty-two hundred miles in circumference. England might be placed in its centre, and its people

could hardly spy the main from its shores. This couplet, however, drew down upon the head of the author very severe rebuke from the British press in after years. The poem was first published complete in America in 1782. Some years afterward it was reprinted in London. In the meanwhile Lord North, who was always near-sighted, had lost his sight entirely, and the critics unfairly imagined that these two lines were intended as a cruel insult. In a subsequent edition, the name of the king was inserted in place of that of North. A few years afterward, the king also was afflicted with blindness. So, to later readers, the unfortunate poet still appeared cruel.

[155] This refers to the confederacy of the Northern European powers against England, commenced in 1780 by the Empress Catharine, of Russia. The ostensible object was to protect the rights of neutrals in time of war—the real object was to cripple the maritime power of England. Catharine issued her proclamation in February. In the course of the summer, Prussia, Denmark, and Sweden, became parties to the policy declared by the Czarina, namely, that no port should be considered blockaded, unless there was sufficient force present to maintain a blockade. In November the States-General of Holland joined the confederacy. France and Spain also acquiesced in the new maritime code, and a general Continental war against England appeared inevitable. This was

called the Armed Neutrality. The scheme failed, however, because of a want of confidence in the faithfulness of the Empress.

[159] This was not uttered in a spirit of prophecy, yet how prophetic were the words, let current history testify. Freneau, another poet of the Revolution, seemed equally prophetic in his *Rising Glory of America*, written in 1775. He says:

―――" I see, I see
Freedom's established reign; cities and men,
Numerous as sands upon the ocean's shore,
And empires rising where the sun descends!
The Ohio soon shall glide by many a town
Of note; and where the Mississippi stream,
By forests shaded, now runs weeping on,
Nations shall grow, and states not less in fame
Than Greece and Rome of old!"

[160] We can never sufficiently lament this sudden termination of the VISION, for it might have extended far down the ages beyond our present experience, and revealed future realities which have not yet become elements of our dreams.

[161] " either tropic now,
'Gan thunder."
Milton's *Paradise Regained*.

[162] The poet here uses a common phrase with the British officers during the war. Every officer who luckily escaped capture or destruction, described his retreat as having " been under the very nose of the enemy."

[163] In allusion to the fact that all obnoxious

New England Tories, when the places of their abode became too hot for them, hastened to Boston, and placed themselves under the protection of the British. M'Fingal, for his loyalty, and for his courage when out of the presence of danger, was as highly deserving of that protection, as his great needs, at that perilous moment, could claim.

[164] Genesis, Chapter xix.

[165] After the Americans had promulgated their Declaration of Independence, the ministerial speakers in parliament, and writers in favor of the government, amused themselves by calling it "The Phantom of Independence." The newspapers echoed the simile, and it was a favorite idea until it assumed a shape so substantial, in the progress of the war, as to make the word ridiculous.

[166] The hegira of M'Fingal, was a memorable epoch in the computation of the Loyalists. Epic poetry has scarcely a parallel in giving the grand catastrophe—the *denouement* of the story. We would gladly tell the reader more of the life of the hero—his sufferings in exile—his promotion in office—his safe denunciations of democracy "under the very nose" of monarchy—but the respectful silence of the poet puts an injunction of secrecy upon the pen of the Annotator.

www.ingramcontent.com/pod-product-compliance
Lightning Source LLC
Chambersburg PA
CBHW030747230426
43667CB00007B/876